How the Shopping Cart
Explains Global Consumerism

How the Shopping Cart Explains Global Consumerism

Andrew Warnes

UNIVERSITY OF CALIFORNIA PRESS

University of California Press, one of the most distinguished university presses in the United States, enriches lives around the world by advancing scholarship in the humanities, social sciences, and natural sciences. Its activities are supported by the UC Press Foundation and by philanthropic contributions from individuals and institutions. For more information, visit www.ucpress.edu.

University of California Press
Oakland, California

© 2019 by The Regents of the University of California

Library of Congress Cataloging-in-Publication Data

Names: Warnes, Andrew, author.
Title: How the shopping cart explains global consumerism / Andrew Warnes.
Description: Oakland, California : University of California Press, [2018] | Includes bibliographical references and index. |
Identifiers: LCCN 2018025164 (print) | LCCN 2018029538 (ebook) | ISBN 9780520968097 | ISBN 9780520295285 (cloth : alk. paper) | ISBN 9780520295292 (pbk. : alk. paper)
Subjects: LCSH: Shopping carts—United States. | Consumption (Economics)—United States. | Shopping—United States. | Merchandising—History.
Classification: LCC HC110.C6 (ebook) | LCC HC110.C6 W37 2019 (print) | DDC 306.3—dc23
LC record available at https://lccn.loc.gov/2018025164

Manufactured in the United States of America

24 23 22 21 20 19 18 19
10 9 8 7 6 5 4 3 2 1

In the fall one walks in the orchards and the ground is hard with frost underfoot. The apples have been taken from the trees by the pickers. They have been put in barrels and shipped to the cities where they will be eaten by people in apartments that are filled with books, magazines, furniture, and people. On the trees are only a few gnarled apples that the pickers have rejected. They look like the knuckles of Doctor Reefy's hand. One nibbles at them and they are delicious. Into a little round place at the side of the apple has been gathered all of its sweetness. One runs from tree to tree over the frosted ground picking the gnarled, twisted apples and filling his pockets with them. Only a few know the sweetness of the twisted apples.

    Sherwood Anderson, *Winesburg, Ohio* (1919)

It is the principle of self-service, at least in the grocery department, which is the *sine qua non* of the supermarket operation. Self-service had, of course, been tried before the advent of the supermarket but never under such Elysian conditions. Through veritable mountains of food, of every variety and description, among thousands of brand names made familiar to her each day by the seductive advertisements of the national magazines, the housewife wanders at leisure without interference. What could be more ideal?

    Max M. Zimmerman, "The Supermarket and the Changing Retail Structure" (1941)

CONTENTS

List of Illustrations ix

Entrance
1

1. Inside Views
19

2. Aristocratic Baskets
26

3. In the Supermarket
46

4. The Late Cart
59

5. Carts Unchained
83

Exit 103

Notes 125
Acknowledgments 145
Bibliography 147
Index 159

ILLUSTRATIONS

1. Cover of *Life* magazine, Special Issue: "Food," 3 January 1955 *4*
2. "Futuristic Supermarket at Expo," 4 May 2015 *11*
3. "Futuristic Supermarket at Expo," 4 May 2015 *11*
4. "Future Food District," 4 May 2015 *12*
5. "Patent for *Self-Serving Store*," 21 October 1916 *35*
6. "Interior of Piggly Wiggly Store," 1918 *36*
7. "Interior of Piggly Wiggly Store," 1918 *37*
8. "Patent for *Combination Basket and Carriage*," 4 May 1937 *63*
9. "Telescope Cart Drawing on Letterhead," 1946 *75*
10. "The New Telescope Cart," ad, 1949 *76*
11. "Shopping in Supermarket," 1957 *99*
12. "Shopping in Supermarket," 1957 *99*
13. Grand Grocery, Lincoln, Nebraska, 1942 *100*

Entrance

This book is about an object that, for many, is fast becoming a thing of the past. Until recently many important voices were calling time on the supermarket cart and associating it with an era of car-based shopping they felt we were leaving behind. At the start of the 2010s these predictions intensified. Market commentators at Goldman Sachs and elsewhere warned the leading supermarkets that they were losing ground to their own online systems, and urged them to pursue an aggressive policy of "capacity exit," and close down their "big-box" superstores on the fringes of suburbia, in order to survive.[1] Those old floodlit warehouses, one *Guardian* columnist noted, were starting to look "horribly antisocial," and especially since rejuvenated street markets and improved offerings online had left shoppers under "less pressure to cram a weekly food shop into a joyless hour."[2] All the while, as leading supermarkets woke up to the fact that the future was turning against them, rumors of Amazon's plans continued to circulate. The launch of Amazon Pantry and other automated food delivery systems ensured that all "brick-and-mortar grocery stores," in the words of one business analyst, remained on "high alert."³

Around 2010 and 2011 many thus felt that the supermarket cart, with its stiff wheels and clanging functionality, was about to fall into disuse. Whatever it might once have explained was now becoming irrelevant. People had already started shopping in other ways. Many had become more interested in the ethics, origins, and healthiness of food, and were finding small independent suppliers far better at catering to their new concerns. Others were shopping online whenever they could. Others still, by 2014 and 2015, were fitting their fridges and kitchen cupboards with Amazon Dash buttons ahead of a time when the Internet of Things would deliver to them all their grocery desires—no doubt via an automated drone—with no need for actual, physical stores again. One thing shoppers were not doing was observing what *Life*'s special issue on American plenty in 1955 had hailed as the new "weekly ritual" of the big supermarket shop.⁴ They were no longer planning meals days in advance, or coaxing their children in and out of child seats, or running off for forgotten items just before the checkout. They were no longer leaning into their carts, heaving them like oil tankers around some suburban ocean of aisles and shelves. Until recently most forecasts thus assumed that such carts were about to go the way of the mixtape or the phonecard, another sudden relic of the modernity just passed. They too seemed scheduled to disappear, fading from the vast administered worlds of the last century even as those worlds withered in turn.

These millennial predictions of the cart's imminent demise often gained in credibility because they seemed to uphold a future long in the making. The dream of a world without shopping carts is almost as old as the shopping cart itself. Even the famous photograph that Arnold Newman took for the cover of *Life*'s special issue implies that the cart had already become a little overfamiliar. Articles inside the magazine itself do laud the American supermarket, eulogizing its achieved vision of "mass luxury" for every "shopper's delight."[5] Already in Newman's shot, however, we find discomfort: a small girl sits wedged into a cart's metal seat, crushing the groceries at her back, a snack already in her hand. We find aversion: her mother, offstage, seems reluctant to follow the cart into *Life*'s world of "mass luxury" and only touches it, and all the jumbled, conflicted demands it contains, with the tips of her leather gloves. Even before the magazine could go on to hail the achievements of American agriculture and technology, *Life*'s cover thus already cast an ambiguous light on the cart, using it to hint at the problems behind the benign promise of plenty.[6] Its overfilled and garish cart certainly evoked a life less comfortable than that led by the young mothers whom we meet inside the magazine itself and who float from aisle to aisle, "pause between nuts and soups," and "gossip amiably" with others while in the company of their children. It hinted at the opposite: that the cart was in fact pulling kin in and pushing kith away, bringing parents and children face-to-face, and recasting the "big shop" as a battle, or protracted negotiation, between them.

Only three years later *Changing Times* magazine could be found scouring the future for alternatives to these ordinary and reusable carts. Anticipating the barcode technology that the National Association of Food Chains would develop in the late 1960s, its editorial predicted that in "another ten years, ... punch-card shopping" would allow "electronic machines [to] select and collect your groceries." Carts would become optional, and any which survived the coming cull would by necessity be "motorized and electronic."[7]

4 / *Entrance*

Figure 1. Cover of *Life* magazine, Special Issue: "Food," 3 January 1955, Arnold Newman.

Over the intervening period, of course, huge social, technological, and cultural upheavals have occurred. Everyday life has "accelerated" beyond measure, threatening our traditional ability to understand "what we are in light of what we are no longer," in Pierre Nora's words.[8] But *Changing Times*' original hope of cart avoidance has remained, throughout this age of acceleration, intact, a mainstay of plans and projections of the future of food shopping. In his predictions for *Advertising Age* in 1994, for instance, Jeffrey Zbar took it as a given that such progress would entail the abolition of store and cart alike. The difference was that this future was now starting to arrive—was already finding an "upscale consumer market" who hoped soon "to whittle the shopping chore down to a few minutes a week on the computer." The clatter and drag of the supermarket cart, for Zbar, would soon fade from memory as customers switched to a new network of "regional distribution facilities" which would "pick-and-pack" their orders via an "interactive TV or computer" before delivering them to their "home or office."[9] Toward the end of the century this much-heralded future was beginning to seem closer still. *USA Today* reported in 1999:

> Throughout greater Boston, more and more households—double income, technologically savvy and greatly pressed for time—are going to their computers to buy groceries rather than to supermarkets. Today ShopLink and three other on-line supermarkets are vying for dominance in greater Boston. The battle for the Boston market may soon be repeated in many other metropolitan areas in the USA. By 2003, on-line grocery shopping is expected to reach $10.8 billion, a surge of 116% from $5 billion now. On the face of it, that sum is hardly enough to rattle the $450 billion supermarket industry. But the explosive growth rate, fueled by consumers' insatiable yearning for convenience, is already attracting major investors to the on-line grocery business....
>
> "It's a time thing," says Meghan Schaney, stay-at-home mom to Nathan, 6, Matthew, 3, and Emilee, 2. "It's a chore from trying to get them in the car, to get them through the store and getting through the chaos when I get back and have to put it away. It would be like a 2-hour ordeal." Schaney, 35, is stop No. 5, and Messier drops off $101 of groceries in less than 5 minutes.[10]

Later press coverage treated all the new innovations of online grocery firms as further steps toward this approaching future. In 1999, when investment from Yahoo, Goldman Sachs, and others allowed Webvan to launch its vision "of supermarket shopping without the supermarket," the *Independent* limited its analysis to asking whether existing technology had really managed to catch up with such a goal.[11] By the time Kosmo.com announced plans to "equip ... every driver with satellite navigation" one year later, the *London Times* was clearly beginning to believe it had.[12] Soon afterward, as these pioneering online ventures folded in turn, each closure was attributed to a kind of overreach, or visionary excess, as if the world was not yet ready for such ideas but would be soon. Left unmentioned was the possibility that the cart was so simple and ingenious that this coming technology would always struggle to replace it.

Sometimes the cart can seem quite invisible in our culture. Sometimes it can seem implicated in a problem—food shopping— it might have been thought to solve, a metonym for docile consumerism, suburban drudgery, or the unpaid labor of modern parenthood. More frequent still are those film and literary narratives from the US and elsewhere which focus on any time but now and anywhere but here—which avoid the ground beneath our feet as though it were more clichéd than the rehashed histories and mystical sagas that they light out for instead. Sometimes it can feel as though the only major American story that really comes to grips with shopping carts is *The Road*, and given that Cormac McCarthy's late novel treats them as just about the only part of our current consumer landscape that can withstand apocalypse, this is a backhanded compliment to say the least. Many of the official plaudits heaped on other modern inventions—and even on such humdrum objects as the safety razor and the revolving door—remain withheld from the cart.[13] Other than its original designers, nobody ever seems to have stood back and admired this new contraption or gasped in wonder at its ingenious design.[14] Even Andy Warhol and Jasper Johns, while busy adapting soup cans and beer bottles for New York's 1961 American Supermarket exhibition, made no attempt to customize the ordinary carts that visitors could push around the gallery's pretend aisles. Our culture in general seems happy to leave them to the homeless.

On the face of it these would seem likely conditions for the further variations on the ancient practice of skeuomorphism that are now proliferating online. *Skeuomorph*, a coinage of the nineteenth century, was invented by classicists and archaeologists to capture the widespread cultural tendency to incorporate decorative allusions to old processes into new forms. Combining the Greek words for "container" (*skeuos*) and "form" (*morphē*), the first *skeuomorphs* were said to be the triglyphs or etchings which appeared in the upper corners of ancient stone temples in Greece and elsewhere and which echoed the joints and dowels of the wooden buildings such stone structures replaced. Yet this skeuomorphic impulse, first identified with the upheavals of ancient cultures, is also proving resurgent today. Many of the pictograms and icons on our PC desktop screens also now echo the functions that they supersede, offering us reassuring continuity at a time of rapid change. As the British novelist Will Self comments:

> It is with the advent of computerised technology that the contemporary obsession with the skeuomorph really gets going.... I remember the first edition of Adobe Page-Maker, which I used in the late 1980s on my Mac Classic computer (remember them? So little and chunky, with the integrated CPU and VDU unit just like an early... television);

when you booted it up you were treated to a graphic showing a medieval monk illuminating a manuscript. Other stand-out computer skeuomorphs include the envelope pictogram employed in numerous email programs, the stylised buff cardboard folders used on desktops (and those "desktops" themselves)—and even aural skeuomorphs, such as the shutter click my iPhone's camera makes as it captures yet another blindingly evanescent image, or the odd whooshing noise it emits when it sends an email.[15]

Whereas the *Oxford English Dictionary* remains noncommittal, only defining the "skeuomorph" as an "ornamental design on an artefact resulting from the nature of the material used or the method of working it," Self here confirms that such "designs" in fact always aim at supplantation.[16] Skeuomorphs, for him, replicate only as they replace: they mimic an existing "method" or "material" precisely so they can eclipse it. Even under his stricter, more aggressive definition, it is clear that Self remains swamped by the wealth of examples he finds beaming back at him from his backlit user screen, and he could easily extend his list far beyond the "stand-out examples" he has chosen. He could have added the silhouetted floppy disk that Microsoft uses for Save, for example, or the Victorian magnifying glass that Adobe uses for Find. He could have included hieroglyphic pencils, erasers, loudspeakers, microphones, tape measures. He could even have mentioned the knife-and-fork logo that Google Maps uses to direct us toward McDonald's among other fast-food stores where cutlery is difficult to find. And he might have also mentioned that at least since Mark Mumma designed an early version of one for his company Real Cart in 1995, the shopping cart icon has appeared a kindred phenomenon.[17] As it now greets us not only on Amazon but on all sorts of organizational homepages, remembers our choices, and guides us toward Checkout, so this ubiquitous pictogram can seem another "anchor," in archaeologist John Blitz's term, mimicking the known and familiar at a time of "rapid change."[18] Certainly, when Jeffrey Bezos patented 1-Click just two years after placing his first cart on Amazon's homepage in 1997, the media response suggested that a new consumer revolution was underway. As it logged bank card details onto the server, allowing customers to fly through checkout by pressing a single button, the sheer speed of Amazon's new shopping system did tend to suggest that technology was now beginning to catch up with an old cultural desire to free ourselves from the raw rudiments of the real-life supermarket shop. And the fact that Bezos cast a simple cart as the public face of this new technology suggests he was indeed aiming for a kind of skeuomorphic outcome—albeit one less playful or accidental than those on Self's list.[19] His choice of a familiar and reassuring cart icon certainly seemed connected to Amazon's wider quest to achieve the old millennial hope of "supermarket shopping without the supermarket."

The trouble is that shopping carts have since proven disobedient "anchors," too useful to submit to such online ornamentalization. All around the world, wherever they have gained a foothold, supermarkets still dominate grocery shopping, and to a large degree they do so because their customers are still pushing actual carts around the actual aisles of actual shops. Memories evoked in other online skeuomorphs are now growing dim. Typographical marks such as ¶ and § now appear the sole domain of Microsoft Word, and most floppy disks still in active use belong to FBI operatives paranoid about hackable online clouds. But the chances are that you will be pushing a cart around a supermarket sometime later this week. Leading cart makers, unlike other US manufacturers, have experienced no significant fall in sales; their annual figures before 2016 contradict the gloomy economic rhetoric of Donald Trump's presidential campaign. Even through a period of low growth some have in fact reported continued expansion, and not least in demand for the double-decker designs familiar to many from Whole Foods and Trader Joe's.[20] Such buoyancy has since encouraged new investment in research and development. The French giant Carrefour revived the 1990s IDEO cart, a prototype which replaces the conventional cage with two rods and overhanging boxes, thus making it a little harder for your old schoolteacher—or whoever it is you would least like to bump into at the checkout—to get a good look at all your tampons and beer.[21] Leading manufacturers in the United States, meanwhile, are now seeking to persuade clients to invest in new carts (which today cost an average of ninety dollars apiece) by offering improved maintenance schemes, protective coatings, and other innovations designed to ensure that their products will endure for much longer than they once did.[22] Carts thus seem destined to remain ubiquitous, in 2-D and 3-D alike, for many years to come. Outright online supplantation remains a distant dream.

Against this background the absence of carts from recent innovations in supermarket design can look less like proof of their imminent demise than the revival of an old attempt to wish them away. The networked "supermarket of the future," which Coop Italy commissioned from the MIT professor and architect Carlo Ratti, for example, gained numerous accolades after it was unveiled at 2015's Milan Expo. Web and print journalists marveled at this new foodscape, many echoing Ratti's own company's publicity and the wonder it expressed at the store's "smart shelves," automated stock replenishment, and the "suspended

Figure 2. "Futuristic Supermarket at Expo," 4 May 2015, Tinxi.

Figure 3. "Futuristic Supermarket at Expo," 4 May 2015, Tinxi.

Figure 4. "Future Food District," 4 May 2015, Antonello Marangi.

digital mirror[s]" on which, as individual shoppers drew near, "extra information" would appear, allowing "each product" to "communicate" to "her" its "nutritional properties, its origin, the presence of allergens, waste disposal instructions, correlated products and promotions and other data, potentially encouraging a stronger use of fresh, local products, and even new social links among people."[23]

To a large extent, however, this tone of excited futurity remained the preserve of the brochure summaries and web reviews which promoted the new design. The photos that accompanied such advertising copy often ran in the opposite direction, revitalizing conventions and even clichés long ago established in the pages of *Progressive Grocer* and among the first US supermarket developers. Here, in empty, gleaming aisles, a cast of young white models can be seen standing and smiling at angled displays of perfect fruit. Reams of bespoke data might materialize before them; holograms might furnish them with nutritional facts and recipe suggestions tailored to their personal dataset. And in other ways the photos might conjure a supermarket from some other world, their glowing foods and smiling faces expressing what the German philosopher Byung-Chul Han has called the new digital ideology of "anesthetic hypercommunication" in which images "lack all brokenness" and "everything that does not submit to visibility" grows doubtful; one dreads to think how actual supermarkets inspired by Ratti's plans might respond to those who ignore their tailored health advice.[24] But as they step through the edible techfest, listening to the algorithm, it also becomes apparent that these models are being asked to look, touch, and choose for themselves in a way that only updates an invitation which Piggly Wiggly and other US businesses first extended to their customers when they replaced their counters with open shelving soon after World War One. In text an emissary of the near future, in image the store remains entrenched in the self-service traditions of old. Ratti even feminizes his clientele. And as he follows the historic example of firms like Piggly Wiggly, luring the hands of his customers into his tilted banks of plenty, it also becomes apparent that he too has found it difficult to allow them somewhere to put all the foods his system has helped them choose. From Piggly Wiggly's Clarence Saunders and other key predecessors, Ratti has inherited the belief that his supermarket displays must be organized around a road-like grid of wide, smooth aisles. But he has also imbibed their reluctance to provide customers with the wheeled carts that his indoor highway all but invites. Unresolved doubts over the cart's place in the future supermarket remain apparent here too.

An unexpected correspondence thus lurks behind Bezos's original skeuomorphic aims and the omissions of Ratti's "supermarket of the future." In trying to forget "real" carts without saying how, the implemented visions of both men remain incomplete, part of a wider commercial culture that seeks the future but cannot quite clear its debts to the twentieth century. Both indeed belong to a new commercial formation in which, instead of the planned incorporation of the 3-D into the 2-D, where the online image would soon only echo an object from yesterday's world, carts increasingly proliferate across both spheres, their "real" and "virtual" modulations echoing each other with undimmed force.[25] The confusion then becomes pronounced as libraries, galleries, museums, universities, government departments, and other public organizations around the world follow Amazon's lead. As they too place carts onto their menu bars, recasting their homepages as "storefronts," they convey that they are no longer providing services but commodities. They "construct and construe" themselves in "market terms," as Wendy Brown puts it, and they present this new transformation as a response to our need for choice and in tones which suggest it is already *"achieved and normative."*[26] Occupying the heart of a digital circuit that folds public and private together, the online cart has thus become a key driver of what Han has called our journey from "citizens into consumers."[27] Colonizing civic life, collapsing our old social vocations under the single appellation *consumer,* its ubiquity now neither surpasses nor ornamentalizes its original referent but endows it with extra force. And there is some irony to be found in the fact that whereas the addition of this online function to public websites often does signal the closure of actual offices and the redundancy of actual staff, the icon which serves as a figurehead of this shift, and which works to place it on the side of technological progress, has never itself usurped its countless 3-D equivalents. Such aberrations might even lead the undifferentiated "consumer" to feel that, for all the talk of an existential competition between them, supermarket and online multinationals alike now together serve what Mark Fisher called "the ultimate cause-that-is-not-a-subject: Capital."[28] As it shuttles between its real and virtual modulations, dragging the world into countless steel and HTTP voids, the cart remains a visible proxy for a global excess we can no longer devolve to individual responsibility.

Under these circumstances, it is perhaps unsurprising that Amazon is now rethinking its initial approach to the shopping cart icon. Far from submitting to a skeuomorphic design, this icon's recent adventures beyond the company's national homepages—its new life as a phone, laptop, and tablet link to the subscription services of Prime—suggest instead a mimicking or appropriation of consumer forces no longer under the multinational's control. Skeuomorphism's latter-day revival, where various technological gains have found their online referents via a successive picturing of loss, finds a limit in the cart's ubiquitous silhouette. As it refuses to become spectral, littering life online as it has long littered "reality" itself, the cart instead recolonizes everyday existence in all its new forms, filling it with real and virtual steel cages that preempt even our more unexpected consumer impulses. This recolonization then intensifies as the cart, rebooted as Prime's official face, now washes back into that prelittered "real" world. As inky 2-D modulations of its online "original" begin to surface on roadside signs and in magazine ads, even appearing on the packaging which now flows out of dark stores dotted around the world, Amazon's acquisition of Whole Foods, and its fleet of physical carts, begins to seem inevitable, part of the bending and dispersal of the original arrow-like line of progress on which Amazon's initial skeuomorphism was based. The 2-D carts on 3-D cardboard which drop into mail boxes worldwide do continue to remind customers of the icons glowing on their smartphone homescreens. But they can also remind them of the empty and expectant button that floats above Bezos's homepage—and they can also bypass both, signifying the ugly cold rows of metal carts which never quite went away. And the twists and turns of this new network of signification confirm that the cart remains at the heart of global consumerism. For all our technocratic dreams of a future without carts, these contraptions remain essential to the final delivery stages in our intercontinental chain of supermarket food flow. It is as though, in the cart's original design, something was unleashed—something which could unsettle even its creators and distributors, but which has allowed our global system to reach new heights of speed and scale, and which the online systems of today can only echo and repeat. For Franck Cochoy and Catherine Grandclément-Chaffy, our leading investigators of the subject, that "something" involves a naturalization of choice and "volumetric" excess. As they put it:

> The shopping cart channels lines and vision into the supermarket aisles. Shopping carts cross without their "pushers" really paying any attention to one another. The cart keeps people's choices in front of them or alongside, and the open basket may be thought of as a vast cavity which ... asks only to be filled. Proof of this is that no one leaves the store empty-handed. Slipping in a coin or token to free up a cart, grabbing hold of the handlebar, is like shaking hands on a contract; it is a tacit agreement to switch status from visitor to buyer.... The cart invites each cluster member to continue putting objects into it until it is full, or "satiated," in what seems an astounding switch from the budget constraints beloved of economists to an extremely generous volumetric one, an oversized technological stomach that can hold up to 240 liters.[29]

The "contract," of course, has no basis in law. Supermarkets, in theory, are open to all. Anyone can "free up a cart," grab "hold of the handlebar," and push it around for as long as they like without buying a thing. If you were to do so, however—if for some strange reason you chose to reenact Allen Ginsberg's "A Supermarket in California" (1956) and went "shopping for images" at your local store, "never passing the cashier"—you would soon feel, as Ginsberg did, that you were attracting the attention of the "store detective" or one of his new nonhuman heirs. Half-hidden CCTV cameras would twitch and pulse at you, flitting between your face and empty cart, deeming you errant, your behavior suspicious. Like Whitman, the "graybeard" confidant of Ginsberg's famous poem, you would thus find yourself shopping "wrong," and not because you were asking "what price bananas?" or "who killed the pork chops?" but because you would be ignoring what Cochoy and Grandclément-Chaffy here cast as the whispered invitation radiating from the expectant, "volumetric" cart. *Fill me. Fill me.* Or perhaps it might be better to say that you would be ignoring all the other voices which the cart allows to speak. *Buy me. Buy me.* For what the cart really provides is the capacity to hear all the enticing sales pitches that issue from the sculpted items which await us in the supermarket's fridges, gondolas, and wall displays. It, more than anything else, is what has allowed us to forget "the salesperson," in David Alworth's words, and to delegate "the function of enticing" to "the commodity package" instead.[30] Simple and expedient, a fillable cavity on wheels, the cart indeed permits us to amass a plethora of these packages at a quick-fire pace. Its yawning void allows us to glimpse and grab, glimpse and grab, generating a heap of goods which is at once an inevitable endpoint of supermarket design and irrefutably *ours*, a materialization of what Tracey Deutsch calls our "elastic, variable, adaptable, uncertain" food choices.[31] Hence the cart "naturalizes" individual overconsumption more efficiently and smoothly than even the most sophisticated web technologies of today ever could. Its simplicity alone, a simplicity impregnated with the moods and capacities of twentieth-century US life, remains integral to shopping online as much as in the mall or on the street.

CHAPTER ONE

Inside Views

The invention of the supermarket cart is on one level basic: a simple story of how modern factories took a prehistoric technology and recast it in steel, producing horizontal rows of simple machines which gave shoppers free rein in the new self-service grocery stores of twentieth-century American life. Alterations in store design over the course of the 1910s and 1920s increasingly allowed customers to shop for themselves, inviting them to pick up branded bottles, boxes, cans, and jars which they would previously have asked for at the counter. As self-service thus "revolutionized the grocery industry," customers needed something large enough to carry all their self-selected items around in— and shopkeepers, fearing a reported rise in shoplifting, needed to ensure that whatever this "thing" was, they could still see into it.[1] At first, as we will see, many food stores responded to these two needs by providing their customers with trays and open baskets. Little by little, however, after the rise of mass car ownership over the 1920s, they began to realize that such modest receptacles were insufficient. Middle-class Americans were now beginning to drive anywhere and everywhere they could—and as their cars came to feature integrated storage compartments, this increasingly included shopping for all the food they needed. As "Car Country quickly became the nation's signature landscape," in the words of Christopher W. Wells, so self-service grocery stores gradually began to consider an in-store response, namely, how to enlarge the transparent cavities that they handed to customers while ensuring they did not become too heavy to carry around.[2] Cars, sprouting trunks, at length meant that baskets sprouted castors, creating an obvious mechanical expedient—a cart—that for the first time allowed customers to fill their trunks and indeed their kitchen cupboards and fridges with enough food to last a week. Unpowered wheels, a simple mechanical advantage known to Neolithic humankind, helped American shoppers to choose their own personal share of the stunning plenitude which other, far more sophisticated networks of agroindustrial production and distribution had deposited in their local grocery store.

The sheer simplicity of these circumstances explains why supermarket carts remain unsung. For many, as I say, these boxes on wheels often do seem lacking in innovation, so much a child of necessity that to speak of them being invented always risks aggrandizing their development. In what follows I will make a case against such skepticism. Later, when I focus on the prototypes which Sylvan N. Goldman, Fred W. Young, and Orla E. Watson developed during the 1930s, I aim to emphasize the ingenuity, the ergonomics or fidelity to human scale, and the long-lasting influence of their work so as to show that these men were nothing if not inventors. But I also accept some of the skepticism that has surrounded their designs, and I do so on the grounds that their somewhat independent inventions were a little late to arrive, adding wheels to baskets and thus "completing" self-service culture decades after its initial emergence. The reasons for the delays in the cart's arrival, as we will see, are as interesting as those behind its eventual invention.

Toward the end of the nineteenth century it became clear that many of the traditional operations of main-street shopping were a source of dissatisfaction for customers and proprietors alike. Novels from a range of different traditions in this period begin to present the old business of ordering your daily needs over a succession of shop counters as a process full of awkward scrutiny and often painful social mediation. All sorts of late-Victorian creatures slope away from these counters in a state of distress, shamed by the exposure of their domestic vices, their need for credit, their hunger, or their inability to afford goods to match the respectability of their speech, manners, or dress. Shopkeepers everywhere thus acquire something of the piercing authority Gustav Flaubert laid bare in his portrait of Artemise Homais, the pompous chemist of *Madame Bovary* (1856). Later novels of urban or industrial life echo the proprietorial power that Homais displays as he clings to the apothecarial scales on his counter—scales Flaubert likens to those above Yonville's court building—and watches over provincial life like "the goldfinch in the wicker cage above his head."[3] In the old Whitby remembered in Elizabeth Gaskell's *Sylvia's Lovers* (1860), for example, the staff of a grocery store all but control their customers, providing them with a "primitive bank," extending or withholding credit, and enthusiastically telling them what they can and cannot afford.[4] It is in American novels, however, from about 1890 onward, that these shopkeepers and their clerks, with their classificatory glances and knowing questions, most often find themselves in competition with new, less interpersonal modes of urban shopping.⁵ Questions fired over old Victorian counters can still probe and discomfort in the work of Theodore Dreiser, for example. Clerks, in control of money, can talk about it in a way that lets them see through formal dress or demure speech to "reveal" the low station of a given hero. Particularly in *Sister Carrie* (1900), however, these inquisitorial shopworkers are also being superseded by the alternatives they shape, the department stores that take a step back from their shoppers, leave them to their own devices, and let them stroll among commodities whose prices are fixed and apparent for all to see. Upon walking into The Fair—a particularly "handsome, bustling, successful affair" in downtown Chicago—Caroline Meeber soon forgets she is looking for work. Instead she becomes lost in her newfound capacity to

> pass along the busy aisles, much affected by the remarkable displays of trinkets, dress goods, stationery, and jewelry. Each separate counter was a show place of dazzling interest and attraction. She could not help feeling the claim of each trinket and valuable upon her personally, and yet she did not stop. There was nothing there which she could not have used—nothing which she did not long to own. The dainty slippers and stockings, the delicately frilled skirts and petticoats, the laces, ribbons, hair-combs, purses, all touched her with individual desire, and she felt keenly the fact that not any of these things were in the range of her purchase. She was a work seeker, an outcast without employment, one whom the average employee could tell at a glance was poor and in need of a situation.⁶

Many have agreed that this is an encounter of some note. In Rachel Bowlby's classic study *Just Looking* (1985), for example, Carrie's passionate longing for the items in front of her becomes leading literary proof of a new "division" between the "access to view and access to possession" which Bowlby discerns in the plateglass windows and other commodity displays of late-

Victorian life.[7] It seems worth noting, however, that whereas *Just Looking* thus fits the passage into an argument about how that metropolitan scene transformed "merchandise into a spectacle," focusing on what Anne Friedberg has called "the indirect desire to possess and incorporate through the eye," the passage itself steps beyond this visual paradigm.[8] Glass, the "transparent substance" and "barrier" at the heart of Bowlby's history, in fact vanishes from this moment of *Sister Carrie*, overtaken by a flurry of tactile formulations.[9] C*ould not help feeling, all touched her, she felt keenly:* Dreiser's language dovetails a great deal more with newspaper reports of the period, echoing their interest in the department store's policy of leaving even expensive stock "lying out invitingly on a counter or showcase" or some other surface in easy reach of clientele.[10] "Each individuated object" on sale here might gain a new and "sensuous appeal," as Bill Brown has suggested.[11] But it is important to emphasize that they do so because Dreiser's hero, unlike her immediate Victorian predecessors, can now move among them, even discreetly touching some in the manner of one who has stepped through the window and entered the display itself.

All the while Dreiser remains wary of the "democratization of luxury" and other "puffery" by which the department stores of the period often promoted their offerings to customers.[12] "Beauty" may well "speak ... for itself" here, to paraphrase the title of a later chapter in his novel.[13] But what it says is not exactly liberating. The articulate "beauty" of each "valuable" instead reaches deep inside, drawing out of customers a commodity desire that leaves them indifferent to those around them. Rich women "brush ... past" Carrie "in utter disregard of her presence," allowing their own spending power to "enlist" them "in the materials which the store contained."[14] *Sister Carrie* treats the department store as a new kind of space, full of atomizing passions, where interhuman relations cede ground to a new communion between shoppers and the objects of their desire.[15]

Desire mesmerizes Carrie too. As a modernizing process here pushes staff to the edge of the store, requiring them to stand back and second-guess a relationship between the consumer and the consumer item that now takes center stage, she is left all but alone to explore these luxury goods for herself. In consequence she gets a taste of what Richard Longstreth has called the "unencumbered" and "nondirectional" mobility which would henceforth characterize American and Americanized shopping, and as she does so she struggles to believe that "patrons" here "may go anywhere in any sequence as often as they choose."[16] Her doubts, however, do not dissuade her from availing herself of these new freedoms. Glances from the "shopgirls" lurking behind the luxury displays do still cause her unease. Dreiser shows that the new organization of commercial space has actually allowed them more scope to stare and assess her "true" status. But he also implies that any disapproval which might now emanate from them can only confirm, can only echo a message Carrie has heard first from the goods themselves. The valuables themselves, overpriced and still a little frightening to touch, have already told her that they are "not...in the range of her purchase."

There is no need for Dreiser to add "yet" to his phrase. The scene itself makes clear that the clerkly sneers and refusals which had once unmasked social impostors, exposing low birth or the stain of poverty, no longer carry the force of a permanent judgment. Carrie instead discovers, in the daunting price of each "valuable," not an eternal prohibition but a negotiable barrier, a challenge which seems only for the time being to prevent her from possessing goods already in her reach. Being so close to the goods, it seems, helps her imagine a way out of her present status as an "outcast," and to experience the "sensuous" encounters of a future version of herself that can actually possess or "own" such surrounding items. Close at hand, she thus experiences these "things" not as forbidden objects from an untouchable sphere, but as grabbable items which swoop near and spin off, arcing toward and then away from her, teasing her in a series of elliptical orbits. And as they thus tantalize her, inviting and refusing forms of touch redolent of ownership itself, they offer Carrie an object lesson in the "perpetual desire[s]" which Walter Benn Michaels has suggested form the basis for a new economy in the novel.[17] They recast price as a barrier between her and her desire; they broaden their appeal to her beyond the visual realm; and then they rehearse possession itself, allowing her to brush against them as if they were already hers. The goods in the department store indeed say a lot; but what they tell Carrie above all is how to shop in the new century.

CHAPTER TWO

Aristocratic Baskets

It is no surprise that in the decades that followed *Sister Carrie*'s publication, the direct encounters with consumer goods at times available in fin de siècle department stores began to spread into other shops and services. The tentative steps such stores had taken toward the coming world of self-service made a great deal of commercial sense. It allowed them, in the words of the slogans that the Alpha Beta stores circulated in 1910s Los Angeles, to "Pile the goods high," "sell them cheap," and "Let the buyer do the work."[1] Opening up their shop displays to customers also allowed them to look ahead to the more "haptic" or multisensory encounters with commodities that would become a commonplace of shopping over the following decades. In the process, as Longstreth comments, they gave a glimpse into an approaching world where those with money could choose "without feeling obliged to buy, without feeling pressure to select quickly, without feeling embarrassed about ignorance of details or about rummaging through an assortment of goods, and without having to wait for service."[2] And as *Sister Carrie* in effect adds, opening stores up for customers also allowed those who did not have such disposable income to imagine their way into future or alternative identities which did, bringing into their multisensory orbits, too, luxury items once forbidden or out of reach. It is no coincidence that forms of personal credit were at the time undergoing significant reorganization and expansion, becoming far less local or ad hoc and far more a source of profit to a modernizing banking sector. As "instalment credit and legalized personal loans" became available for the first time, the prospect of a direct sensory encounter with consumer goods ensured that the fall in sales some feared would result from the move toward self-service never came to pass.[3] Sensual proximity to desirable items would in time prove more than a match for any upselling or other acts of persuasion that could be carried out by the shop clerks associated with the previous commercial formation.

Most US store owners in the 1910s and 1920s found the optimized psychological capacities of self-service a lot less tangible than all the new efficiencies it offered. Some contemporary retailers replaced counters or installed open shelves or otherwise followed the trend toward self-service because they wanted to seem modern and face the future. Some, too, were led in this direction by the packaging itself, by the bottles, boxes, cans, and jars now wrapped in bright bold print, and by the introduction of standard logos and lettering which increasingly caught the eye on billboards and in newspapers and drew it toward "the talking signs" and colorful items waiting inside the store itself. (In the 1910s, like many other leading-brand manufacturers of the era, Kellogg's began to incorporate color images of its boxed products into its ads as a matter of course; another aid to brand recognition arrived as these ads "spoke" to customers directly, bidding them "Good Morning!" before urging them to look out for their owner's signature when scanning the grocery store shelves.)⁴ But whether they sold clothing, dry goods, groceries, hardware, or toys, all of the stores which thus gravitated toward self-service also did so because it gave them new scope to reduce labor costs. As food historian Lisa Tolbert notes, "clerk wages... were typically one of the largest overhead expenses" for all shop owners in this period. All kinds of developments after 1900, from the proliferation of new cash registers which "would ultimately systematize accounting procedures" to the arrival of "signs and price tags and product packaging [which] took over the informational role of the clerk," gave them all kinds of opportunities to chip away at this sizeable line in their budget.⁵

Many store owners leapt at the chance. With every passing year over the 1910s, their interest in easing their dependence on wage labor became more urgent. The approaching war would take many young men out of the labor pool; those left were not unaware of the considerable progress the trade union movement had made in its fight to improve pay and curb the length of the working day.⁶ Women working in the original department stores remained un-unionized in this period. But successful strikes in the textile factories which supplied them, and the Women's Trade Union League's success in offering representation to other kinds of female-dominated work, left managers worried that their staff, too, would soon collectivize and agitate for better conditions and pay.⁷

These worries had a mixed effect on the luxurious trappings which had long been the hallmark of the department store. By the 1910s, as Susan Benson has shown, the female clerks of such stores had developed a professional sales culture and took pride in their mastery of an exacting mode of service in which they stood back and intuited before they drew out and guided the consumer impulses of wandering clientele. But for managers listening in for rumors of union organization, this professionalism could feel like something of a mixed blessing. Clearly it offered a great boon to customer service and could be talked up in publicity as further proof of the bespoke and almost reverential attention that their recherché stores lavished upon individual shoppers. But such businessmen also believed that promotional tributes of this kind carried a dangerous acknowledgment. It overpaid the underpaid, at least in the currency of words, conceding that they were functioning at a far higher level than *Sister Carrie*'s gossipy "shopgirls" and that they were indeed a professional workforce as deserving of decent conditions as any group of working men.[8] Managers of department stores thus became ambivalent about the skills of their own staff at the same time as the "nondirectional" mobility that their commercial sector had pioneered was being adopted and amplified in other kinds of stores where it was often cast as a culture of self-service and associated with reduced labor costs. Of all the innovations of the fin de siècle department store, what really endured was not a new professional culture of discreet and subtle selling—was not its clerks' erstwhile capacity to ascertain "a woman's size" and "the cost of the outfit she wore" without saying a word—but the underlying structure which these Holmesian habits of instant assessment reflected: the open spaces that allowed customers to wander, linger, and even feel potential purchases for themselves.[9]

Haptic commodity encounter, or what Roland Barthes once spoke of as consumerism's "tactile phase of discovery," thus began to outgrow its original association with the opulent department store as dramatized in *Sister Carrie*.[10] In the years after Armistice, as Tolbert suggests, the average "self-service store ... turned out to be a small and intimate affair," purveying dry goods or groceries, "in stark contrast to the luxurious finishes," elevators, and escalators of Marshall Field in Chicago or Macy's in Manhattan or any of the other legendary downtown department stores which still draped their vision of "democratized" luxury across entire city blocks.[11] And over the same period, some of these famous department stores changed, too, and in some ways became a little more like the supermarkets we know today. As the 1920s progressed, in the words of Longstreth, the "role of the sales clerk as an intermediary between customer and wares became diminished" at the same time as many stores exchanged the maximized "perimeter glazing" and "skylit atria" of the 1890s for "improved lighting systems and air conditioning" which supported "internally focused layout systems designed to enhance the presentation of merchandise and human circulation."[12] In a parallel development, meanwhile, more and more grocery stores up and down the United States introduced enticing and touchable commodity displays and other self-service touches, becoming more like department stores even as the department stores, still expanding and in some cases overexpanding, became more like the supermarkets of a later urban phase. A pioneering example of one such emporium was described at length in the *New York Times* as early as December 1917:

> A grocery store in Lockport, N.Y., is making a novel use of the self-service idea. The Modern Merchant and Grocery World gives the following description of how it is utilized there:
> "A customer enters the store through a turnstile, the purpose of which is merely to register the number of persons who enter each day. Here the customer helps herself to a tray which looks very much like a long pan with two handles on it, or, if she prefers, a regulation market basket. There is no charge for this pan-like container, which is simply a convenience for gathering up the items the housewife selects. If, on the other hand, she wishes to use a basket

in which to carry her goods home she is charged 4 cents for it, which amount she receives on returning it.

"Shelves are indexed alphabetically, beginning with 'A,' as one enters the store, and on these shelves one finds the commodities beginning with the particular initial letter—for instance, under 'A' there are ammonia, asparagus, apricots, &c. A low partition divides the store. A customer walks down one side and up the other, selecting the goods she desires. When she has finished with the letter 'X Y Z' she finds herself at the cashier's desk, where she takes her purchases out of the pan, or basket, and the cashier checks the items and collects the amount. If the customer has been using a pan to collect the groceries she proceeds to the front of the store, where a large shelf is placed for the accommodation of those desiring to wrap their packages, paper and string being provided for this purpose. When this is done the customer returns the pan to the cashier's desk; if a basket is used she does not bother with the wrapping, but merely takes her purchases home. Every article in the store is plainly marked with the price at which it is sold.

"A store manager is in charge, and, in addition to the cashier, has a clerk to assist. The proprietor and the clerk do nothing but fill up the shelves to get things ready for the selling hours."[13]

Quoted in the original "newspaper of record," the advertorial for the Modern Merchant and Grocery World takes the form of a lesson: how, at the apex of the Progressive Era, one might go shopping for food. By necessity, as it does so, its lauding of the newest business in Lockport often yields to an explanation of its commercial innovations, while these explanations in turn often become a little defensive in tone.[14] Our anonymous voice, having captured the *New York Times* as its temporary mouthpiece, hopes to fix attention on the transparency, efficiency, and other modern features which the small-town business has imbibed from places like Hengerer's, a modern, multistory department store at the time doing good business thirty miles away in downtown Buffalo.

It assures readers that in Lockport, too, "every article" will be "plainly marked with the price at which it is sold." The imagined customer here too will gain a new dominion over the store overall, looking over its "low partition" and selecting all "the goods she desires." The new approach promises to leave behind the congested city markets and "canny gaze" of the old store counter which, as Tracey Deutsch has shown, continued to dominate food shopping in the United States in the 1910s and 1920s.[15]

Yet it soon becomes apparent that this new shop is offering only a partial rendition of the "nondirectional" mobility beginning to be available elsewhere. A commitment to rational transparency vindicated in the department stores' successful use of clear fixed pricing here surges beyond that commonsensical measure and persuades the new business to organize its entire range of merchandise according to the abstractions of the alphabet. To encounter this kind of arrangement would probably feel quite bewildering to us today. It would be an interesting supermarket in 2019 that placed diluted ammonia right next to asparagus. And these asparaguses, like the apricots, are canned. Any chance such alphabetization ever had of catching on would clearly never survive what Susanne Freidberg has called the "cold revolution" of the late 1920s.[16] Once electric refrigerators became a familiar sight in food stores as well as domestic kitchens, questions of freshness and perishability would clearly supplant such contrived modes of ordering store groceries.

But perhaps the *Modern Merchant and Grocery World*'s peculiar organization of goods never caught on not because it felt odd or inappropriate but because it was too clear—too transparent and easy to follow. Any customers pushed for time could easily alphabetize their shopping list in advance, preplanning their quickest route through the new store. Only first-time visitors would really have shopped "nondirectionally," shuttling from haptic shelf to haptic shelf in that listless state in which (as supermarket planners would soon discover) food shoppers become likeliest to buy stuff on impulse.[17] And it seems likely that anyone who failed to follow the store's alphabetical route, or who wandered around as dazed and confused as Carrie in The Fair Store, would soon catch the attention of the clerk whose only named duties here take place outside business hours. Indeed, if we feel that the advertorial is a bit too keen to insist that "the purpose" of "the turnstile ... is merely to register the number of persons who enter each day," then it might also seem to us that the clerk who is said to "do nothing" besides "filling up the shelves to get things ready for the selling hours" in fact has plenty of other work to occupy his time. *Is there nothing else in your basket? But you only paid for one.* Obvious overstatements and omissions in the advertorial suggest that the patient habits of silent ascertainment which had reshaped customer service on the floor of the department store are here being recast in the name of surveillance. The clerk and the counter are withdrawing to the edges of the grocery store, yet they leave behind new suspicions about theft and a new anxiety that the customer has been handed too much freedom. Lost human control, the price of modernity, continues to haunt the progressive scene, rematerializing in covert but unsubtle antitheft structures.[18]

The store, then, is taking a leap into the unknown. Open and enticing, it is allowing customers to come face-to-face with the vibrant advertising that by now covered the skin of most leading commodities. But in the process it fears that it is unleashing new impulses, not just to consume but to consume more than you can afford, and that it is creating new opportunities to hide such excessive consumption from view. Not unlike the turnstile and the clerk, both the "regulation" basket and the complimentary "tray which looks very much like a long pan with two handles on it" would thus appear to exceed their stated function of helping the housewife "gather ... up the items [she] selects." Both objects act on her in other ways as well—on ways which already point toward the carts that stores would only begin to adopt well over twenty years later. Basket and tray alike indicate a new capacity, offering predetermined cavities big enough to teach this anticipated customer that her selections in the store should be multiple, abundant, and range around all the different goods, from fruit to cleaning products, that it has placed within her reach. But both these objects at the same time enforce transparency. Replacing personal bags and baskets with their standardized in-store equivalents ensures that all her choices from these stacks of plenty will remain in clear sight of the proprietor and clerk even as they continue to "do nothing but fill up the shelves."

Similar developments were at the time taking place nine hundred miles to the south in Tennessee. Only months before Lockport's Modern Merchant and Grocery World placed its ad in the *New York Times*, the entrepreneur Clarence Saunders filed the first of several patents modeled on the Piggly Wiggly store, which he had recently opened on Memphis's Jefferson Street. Indeed, while his title hailed his invention of a "self-serving store," his patent's subsequent wording effectively conceded that this "invention" had already gained a foothold in daily life and that Saunders was only offering some "new and useful Improvements" to it. Even these "Improvements," moreover, largely adapted existing innovations. The obvious precedent of the department store inspired him as it had his counterparts in upstate New York. His patent, too, opened his shop to customers, jettisoning the

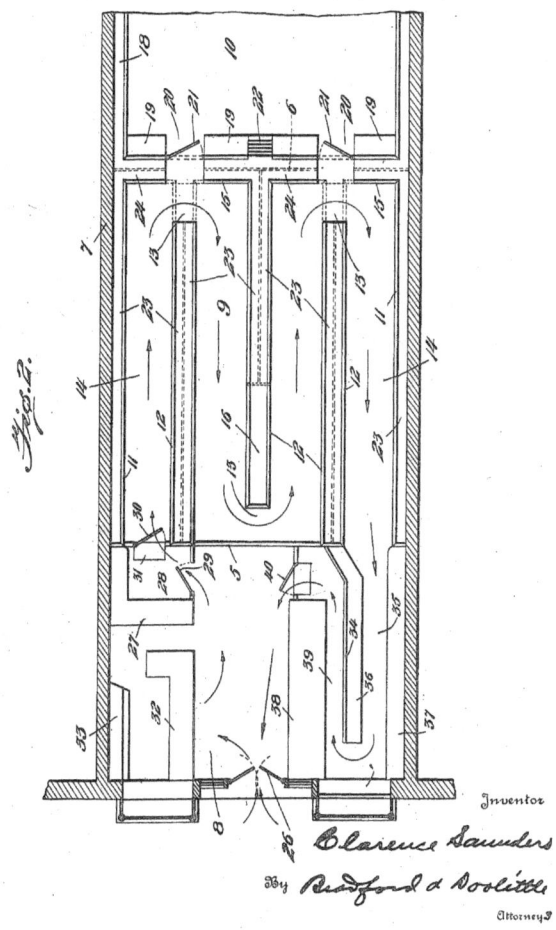

Figure 5. "Patent for *Self-Serving Store*," 21 October 1916, Clarence Saunders.

Figure 6. "Interior of Piggly Wiggly Store," 1918, Clifford H. Poland.

daunting counter of old and allowing them to reach into the "freestanding shelving units" along his aisles.[19] But as he arranged these aisles into a grid layout, Saunders's patent paid an equally direct tribute to the automobile network then being formalized in downtown Memphis among other metropolitan areas. Discouraging backward steps, his requirement that customers follow a "continuous circuitous path" around his store was perhaps not inventive so much as a literal, indoor nod to the new laws and protocols then beginning to control the traffic outside.[20] Even his patent's euphemistic retention of a "floor-walker" who would patrol the deserted store, "inspecting the amount of stock on

Figure 7. "Interior of Piggly Wiggly Store," 1918, Clifford H. Poland.

hand without interfering with" paying customers, recalls surveillance practices also developed in Lockport, New York, and elsewhere.

Saunders never quite allowed himself to harness the full potential of his own creation. For all the visits he made to the Patent Office and for all the franchises he sold to rival firms, the inventions he claimed for himself were ultimately less noteworthy than his knack for imagining a new and important current in American cultural life. It was his understanding of consumer flow—his feel for his customers' desire for a clean and hygienic store where they could shop all but anonymously—that really led others to anoint him the architect of self-service. Convenience, the watchword of his patents, was for him an unlikely source of heroism, a way of bringing respite to the female shoppers in his mind. His stores might have continued to sell some items loose or over the counter. As Warren Belasco has noted, however, the mission of his 1920s "groceterias" was to minimize the "interpersonal contact or negotiation" that such traditional purchases still necessitated and to "maximize impulse purchases" occasioned by his customers' direct encounter with his goods.[21] His 1917 patent even went so far as to specify that the doors of his fridge cabinets should feature "self-closing hinges," sparing his shoppers the hassle of having to push them shut.[22] Through this and a hundred other details, both in the patent and the subsequent running of his stores, Saunders placed the seductive promise of convenience before his customers. As one of his early ads suggested, they flocked to his stores because

> They know they can select exactly what they want, not what somebody wants to hand them. No one to persuade, no one to suggest, no one to recommend what they shall or shall not buy.
>
> They know that at Piggly Wiggly they will not have to wait until Mrs. Extra Fussy, or Mrs. Can't Quit Talking, or Mrs. Perpetual Grouch have been waited on.
>
> They know that they save money. They know that they save time. They know that they get clean goods from a clean store.[23]

Another early ad explained:

> Piggly Wiggly knows its business and its business will be this: To have no store clerks gab and smirk while folks are standing around ten deep to get waited on. Every customer will be her own clerk, and if she wants to talk to a can of tomatoes and kill her time, all right and well—and it seems likely this will be a mighty lonesome chat.[24]

At the heart of Saunders's vision was an ideal shopper—an imagined white housewife of virtue and grace. His early ads for Piggly Wiggly followed the lead of Kellogg's among other leading-brand producers insofar as they too "talked" to such women directly, sometimes addressing them as individuals and sometimes as a collective group. But this way of addressing an optimal clientele was delicate and complex. Conjuring up an identity in the act of addressing it, it at once elided and sought to transcend an existing situation in which food shopping across the Jim Crow South often actually took place in the mixed "commercial space" of "the urban grocery store," where "white and black, rich and poor, men and women interacted on a daily basis."[25] Saunders's regular commercial pitches to what Elizabeth Abel has called that "most intensively policed, yet insistently reiterated conjunction, white women," effectively promised to lift them out of an awkward and unpredictable commercial culture and deliver them into a space based on the curbing of social encounter of all kinds.[26] His notions of what might or might not appeal to this imagined constituency then shaped many of the modifications he made to his original business template—and these modifications in turn exerted profound influence over supermarket design for generations to come. The ideal white housewife whom Saunders conjured before his own eyes deserved to shop at her own pace; so he tempered his original prohibition of backward steps, assuring new customers they could just "shop slowly or quickly" and coming to grasp that "fine ideas for dishes and menus keep bobbing up when you shop this way."[27] But this customer would also, of course, want any store she frequented to be as clean and bright and orderly as her own home; so, having first made sure that they were "empty of customers," he commissioned photographs of his stores designed to emphasize their cleanliness and visual order. White tile floors gleam in the lobby. Canned goods containing like products grouped together are stacked in rigid uniformity on shelves. Modern refrigerators display perishables. Customers were attracted to the clean, orderly environment of the self-service grocery.... Modern amenities such as electricity, refrigeration, and cash registers added substantially to merchants' overhead costs but increasingly were considered essential to attract middle-class white female trade.[28]

Such statements confirm that Saunders was following a circular logic. Imagining food shopping as a "gendered practice," as Tolbert points out, he continually endeavored to accommodate "particular motivations" which he "ascribed" to the ideal white housewife in his head.[29] Many of these ascribed "motivations" were explicit. The imagined white women to whom he presented his stores wanted to be "free from suggestions or persuasion," to shop at their own pace, and to encounter, even at the checkout, only minimal delay. Other "motivations" perhaps went without saying. Traditional shop counters, a source of painful social scrutiny elsewhere, could feel even uglier in a southern region officially determined to keep the races apart. Many small grocery stores installed signs in the form of arrows that pointed African Americans toward separate lines which clerks would turn to only after they had served all their white customers. Others achieved a similar effect by introducing a simple rope and tolerated conversation across this barrier only if it was initiated from the white side. But all of those businesses which could "not afford not to sell to African Americans," in Abel's words, likewise relied upon a painful or embarrassing situation which laid bare the injustice and torturous racial protocols of the region.[30] In his commercial presentation of Piggly Wiggly, then, Saunders clearly sought to offer his imaginary white women much more than an alternative to "the disorganized sights and smells of old-fashioned grocery interiors."[31] He also promised an escape from what Hale has called the "messiness" and "problem" that remained characteristic of food shopping in the region.[32] Because he courted wealthy customers while urging even those with black staff to shop for themselves, the new kind of shopping experience of his commercial rhetoric was at once modern and exclusive, a de facto refuge from the symbolic violence of Jim Crow as well as from the racist fear of racial difference. The fact that the boxed goods inside featured so many caricatures of smiling black "spokesservants," from Aunt Jemima to Uncle Ben, confirmed that Saunders was offering a new and (commercially speaking) "progressive" channel for the unfettered daily pursuits of white privilege.[33]

The image of an ideal white housewife, then, inspired Saunders to introduce a range of improvements that would have a lasting impact over the US grocery sector, flooding his stores with smooth-tiled surfaces, "nondirectional" movement, and geometric stock displays. In the process, however, Saunders also generated tensions of his own. His ideal customer was, as I say, a walking picture of feminine grace. In numerous Piggly Wiggly ad campaigns during the 1920s she stands alone before some immaculate line of canned goods, a smile on her face, an unfilled basket perched on her arm. The captions of such images make it clear that for all her newfound powers of self-selection it remains somehow difficult for this mythic creature to describe her own desires. Estranged from her own stomach, she can only plan meals for her children or look out for favorite family brands for her husband to eat. Some thirty years earlier Thorstein Veblen had written of his hope that industrial society was moving away from an "ideal of feminine beauty" that had long prized "the infirmly delicate, translucent, and hazardously slender." He yearned for an end to that "archaic type" of mythic "woman" who was required to "disown her hands and feet" among "the other gross material facts of her person."[34] In the fuller figure of Saunders's ideal housewife, as pictured in various 1920s ad campaigns and beauty contests, that earlier hope is fulfilled to some degree. Photos and illustrations confirm that her "waist" is not so slender as to imply "extreme debility," and her hands seem set free, attracting attention as they close in on some new and gleaming display. When she reaches out to choose this or that grocery item, however, she always does so with someone else in mind. Never acting on her own appetites, she remains insulated, not just from the outside world of race and difference but also from the tremors and pangs of hunger inside her own mind. The new cultural system that Saunders based on immediate human impulses thus has a hollow agent at its heart. The men in Saunders's cultural system "can eat *and* be loved," in Susan Bordo's words.[35] But the solitary woman whom his ads encounter in his stores remain figures of "ideal beauty and slenderness," selfless if not "translucent," unable to step outside their role as wives and mothers.[36]

These fantasies limited Saunders's ability to make full use of the new capacities that his own designs had created. On the one hand, he still sought to expand his self-service franchise wherever possible. His fixation on the needs of an imaginary white housewife did not stop him from opening a store on Memphis's Beale Street for an African American clientele. Newspaper reports from the late 1920s also indicated he hoped to open a hundred new stores in Australia and New Zealand, and at this time in general he was working to fulfill the ambitious slogan *All over the World*, which he had added to his store signs earlier in the decade.[37] As he did so, however, he also vied for the custom of rich white women in a way that at once ignored other groups and limited his scope for bringing about a further expansion of sales.[38] His punning appeals to "High Heel Society" and his attempts to establish a new "Aristocracy of the Market Basket" all signaled that the dictates of respectability were taking precedence over other considerations. His hopes of cultivating what Marcie Ferris has called a "bright, efficient, sanitized shopping experience" were now eclipsing his capacity to exploit the possibilities for discount and large-volume sales that his own self-service model had opened up.[39]

Such possibilities Piggly Wiggly now left for others to explore. Venturing beyond luxury, Ralphs in Los Angeles, and Michael Cullen's King Kullen in Queens above all, now began to push volume sales, reprising Alpha Beta's old mantra "pile it high and sell it cheap."[40] Cullen in particular sought to carve out what he called "monstrous stores, ... about forty feet wide and a hundred and thirty to a hundred and sixty feet deep, ... with plenty of parking space."[41] By 1940 *Fitch's List of Super-Markets*, for one, included in its catalogue any "retail self-service grocery store having 5,000 square feet with annual sales of $250,000 or over."[42] (In 1941 the leading industry champion Max M. Zimmerman used a similar definition to suggest that the number of supermarkets in operation in the United States had risen from 1,200 in 1936 to 7,980 at the end of the decade.[43]) As such giant stores first became reality and then became the norm, Piggly Wiggly left it to others, too, to realize that old "market baskets," however "aristocratic," were no longer quite enough.

King Kullen especially, less gallant, less beholden to the niceties of gender, took the self-service template that Saunders had pioneered, and developed and expanded it until it met all "five criteria" that for the Smithsonian Institution "define the modern supermarket: separate departments; self-service; discount pricing; chain marketing; and volume dealing."[44] Even after Cullen's sudden death in 1936 his supermarkets continued to push their "monstrous," seductive formula out of the New York suburbs and deep into Long Island. Eventually dropping Cullen's original preference for curbside parking over dedicated parking lots, they pushed ever eastward, following the new parkways that Robert Moses was opening amid great public acclaim.[45] As they did so, opening new branch stores in Huntington, Lindenhurst, Patchogue, and Port Jefferson, they created new traffic flows between Moses's cloverleaf and "jug-handle" junctions and the parking lots that they now began to place outside each new store.[46] They, like leading Californian retailers of the time, presented customers with what Longstreth has described as a new "opportunity to pull off the street, park adjacent to the store, and have purchases placed in the car by an attendant," in the process affording new parallels between their easy, fluid shopping environments and the fledgling automobile network outside. Trade pamphlets would soon be advising new grocery outfits to forgo "turnstiles" and avoid "congestion," to take pains to "promote an easy flow of traffic through the entire store."[47] In Louisville, Kentucky, as Belasco has noted, one business even experimented with an "automarket" concept in which shoppers could simply remain in their cars and drive through the "grocery-lined interior streets."[48] Even across all ordinary experiences of grocery stores, the debt to car culture was rarely difficult to see. In the middle decades of the twentieth century, as Marshall Berman observed, a "new order" began to "integrate ... the whole nation into a unified flow whose lifeblood was the automobile," and the realm of food shopping was no exception.[49] Aisles leading into supermarket checkouts could suggest a "toll booth's drive-up lanes," as Emanuel

Halper noted; new poster campaigns could mirror the billboards at the side of the road; and anyone who in talking to a friend or looking for some elusive item held up their fellow shoppers could soon find themselves on the receiving end of mutters or sighs among other human equivalents of the car horn.[50] What Longstreth calls the new "couplet" of the "nondirectional" store and "nondirectional" parking lot was thus heaving into view. Only a few years later their combination would seem "mundane," a feature of suburban life many had already learned to overlook.[51]

The trouble was that even late into the 1930s, this new and familiar "couplet" lacked a rhyme. Neither Piggly Wiggly's "market baskets" nor the "attendants" and "grocery boys" who spent their lives trudging from checkouts to car trunks formed anything like a modern or progressive "echo" of all the Fords, Buicks, and Oldsmobiles parked outside. Respectively revealing a residual reliance on visible human labor and limiting purchases to what customers could carry, such grocery boys and such baskets alike marked a limit in the supermarket's determination to bring self-service to its logical endpoint. At a time of intense competition between rival firms, both reminded shopkeepers and shoppers themselves that shoppers could not actually go ahead and grab absolutely everything they wanted before transferring it to their car trunks by their own lights.[52] A new commercial world, a world based around the new conveniences of driving, thus pulsed ahead, inchoate but growing in strength. It took a simple indoor replica of the car, stripped down to the wheel and trunk, to complete it.

CHAPTER THREE

In the Supermarket

Sometimes even the historians of everyday objects can begin to believe that everyday life is trivial or lacking in interest. As they dig into the history of this or that topic, from the Lego brick to the humble shopping cart, the unexpected influences that they uncover can persuade them that the object in their sights is not so ordinary after all, but fundamentally unlike all those other "quotidian" materials which still seem inflated by that elegant Latin euphemism. Even they can thus exhibit what Henri Lefebvre described as the intellectual habit of lifting our own interests onto a higher plane, and of considering everyday life as "residual, defined by 'what is left over,'" and bereft of the fertile matter we ourselves remove from it.[1] Since Lefebvre's death in 1991, Bruno Latour's analyses of the actual day-to-day interactions of humans and objects have offered a powerful defense against such reductive habits. Latour has emerged as a "Prince of Networks," in Graham Harman's phrase, who asks "how things interact on a local level without appealing to some all-powerful super-entity that's somehow hidden from us."[2] It thus seems important, given this essay's underlying interest in how the shopping cart has transformed shopping, to spend a few moments here considering Latour's way of thinking about the relationship between objects and human behavior.

Such considerations sometimes simplify Latour's thought. Critical glosses often now speak of his "flat ontology," a phrase meant to capture his belief that "we" do not just use objects but are also used by them, our actions always being shaped by the possibilities they place before us. But the starkness of such summaries can imply that Latour's key analytical figures—the *human* and *nonhuman actants* within a given network—exist in utter opposition to each other. As such it is worth remembering that Latour elsewhere critiques antinomies, seeking the "no-man's land" between the "Nature pole and the Subject pole."[3] If Mohandas Gandhi and Martin Luther King Jr. called their activism *nonviolent* rather than *passive* because they wanted to show that they were only channeling the political anger of their followers, then the weak negation of Latour's *nonhuman* marks a similarly thin and porous distinction.[4] Latour, in rhetoric often differentiating his key categories, in practice as often emphasizes all the properties they hold in common. He shares Jane Bennett's feeling that the "I" is made of "It," along with her sense that the "outside-that-is-inside" us is hidden by our anthropocentric image of ourselves in opposition to external matter.[5]

Recognizing this anthropocentric image, and how it hides the common properties of the human and nonhuman, holds the key to our understanding of the supermarket. When Latour first mentions such stores, admittedly, he remains quite conventional. *Reassembling the Social* (2005) drags them into a critique of academic specialization, likening those scholars who focus on a single theme to grocery shoppers who zoom in on one aisle and ignore the supermarket's other offerings.⁶ But this metaphoric figure later becomes the ground for a direct analysis; and as he faces it head on, Latour finds in the supermarket an epitome of what he calls "subscription." He suggests that such new stores are different because they counterpoise compulsion and choice to "bewildering" effect. The supermarket, he says, wants to "preformat ... you to be a consumer, only a generic one ... with an ability *to calculate* and *to choose.*" To this end its new commercial "topography" contains "plug-ins" that you can

> download on the spot to *become* locally and provisionally competent.... If you look at supermarkets in this way, a bewildering array of devices is underlined, each having the capacity to provide you with the possibility of carrying out calculations somewhat more competently. Even when one has to make the mundane decision about which kind of sliced ham to choose, you benefit from dozens of measurement instruments that equip you to become a consumer—from labels, trademarks, barcodes, weight and measurement chains, indexes, prices, consumer journals, conversations with fellow shoppers, advertisements, and so on. The crucial point is that you are sustaining this mental and cognitive equipment as long as you *subscribe* to this equipment.⁷

Here, although less hostile than a later interview in which he agreed that the supermarket "is all manipulation," the "place you hate most of all," Latour is certainly ambivalent.⁸ David Alworth in fact suggests that in Latour's view of the supermarket, "the human subject is not only one of the many actants constituting the network but is itself constituted by the nonhuman objects ... , the 'bewildering array of devices' that buzz and jingle in every aisle and on every shelf."⁹ Yet while this might seem to overstate matters, implying that human agency had flourished outside the "nonhuman" supermarket only to be liquidated inside it,

Alworth's bleak scenario remains rooted in the skepticism he finds in *Reassembling the Social* itself. Under the terms of Latour's own analysis, supermarkets do conspire against individual variation, recognizing us far less as people than as genres; Latour himself does channel the hostility that was widespread among those earlier European critics who had witnessed the arrival of such stores from the United States after 1945 and who, on the whole, disliked what they saw. His skepticism chimes with the attacks on the supermarket's "superabundance" and "proliferation of kitsch" to be found in Jean Baudrillard's *The Consumer Society* (1970), for example. It makes common ground with Giorgio Agamben's *Infancy and History* (1993), a work which salutes these stores as a "Land of Cockayne" only to indict them for a "dumb promiscuity" which ushers in what Agamben calls the "destruction of experience."[10] Latour's analysis might even recall the Clash's "Lost in the Supermarket" (1979): the celebrated lyrics Joe Strummer wrote for Mick Jones do gesture toward subscription ("I came in here for a special offer") before describing a kind of surrender, a yearning to reach out and grab a "guaranteed personality," the "I" again disappearing amid its own opted manipulations.[11] Continuities then do link Latour with his despondent European predecessors. He might stop short of upholding Erich Fromm, Theodor Adorno, and Max Horkheimer's dire 1940s warnings of a new "schema of mass culture" which would organize "even the most intimate impulses of its forced consumers" into received generic categories and create a new "economic apparatus ... without the hindrance of individuation."[12] But his elaborations on the supermarket's "plug-ins" still amount to a numb echo of such Frankfurtian fears. For Latour, too, grocery stores, long championed in the pages of *Life* and elsewhere as a leading achievement of capitalistic individualism, in fact push us all toward stereotypes, absorbing us into this or that existing subset of behavior.

What distinguishes *Reassembling the Social*, then, is its sheer detail—the attention it pays to the supermarket itself. For Baudrillard and Agamben, and perhaps for Strummer too, the supermarket is a metonym, a knowable stand-in for capitalism's centerless global operations.[13] Its "slot machines and credit cards," for them as for Marc Augé, "communicate" with us "wordlessly" and "through gestures," connecting us with "abstract, unmediated commerce" in "a world...surrendered to solitary individuality."[14] Yet where these critiques treat the supermarket as a shorthand for systems outside its own four walls, Latour remains focused on the world inside the store itself. Like Franck Cochoy, he recognizes that the "interobjectivity" of the average supermarket trip remains organized around the "heart and mind" of individual shoppers; like the British geographer Daniel Miller, he recognizes that these shoppers' choices often translate into "acts of love" toward those left at home.[15] Loath to appeal to what Harman called an "all-powerful super-entity" and wondering, perhaps, whether "commerce" is ever really "unmediated," he thus catalogues all the "labels" and "trademarks," "barcodes" and "conversations," which shape individual choice to form supermarket experience as opposed to its Agambenian nullification. Without asking us to love the supermarket, Latour urges us to keep on studying it—to understand even the oldest and most "naturalised" aspects of its commercial operation.

When we do this in a historical manner, attempting a holistic view of the supermarket system as it emerged in Tennessee, Long Island, and Los Angeles at the end of the 1930s, a number of interlinked aspects become apparent.

It becomes apparent that even the legendary stores of Clarence Saunders and Michael Cullen were only links in a chain. They were just duplicates, and both in the sense that they were just examples of a formula that these entrepreneurs were repeating across their local hinterlands, and because they were mere conduits in a wider network of domestic food distribution which Frank Norris had already likened to a "flood" of "primeval energy" in 1903 and which, for all the shocks of depression and war, had continued growing ever since.[16] Annual US wheat production, Norris's chief concern in *The Pit* (1903), already stood at 683,927,000 bushels in 1909 and then rose steadily, despite the bad harvests of 1934 and 1935, to reach 1,457,435,000 bushels in 1958 before almost doubling again in the 1990s.[17] The growth in sugarcane was perhaps even more important. It was certainly steeper. Thanks in large part to the mechanical sugarcane harvesters that became available between the wars, US production rose from 4,884,000 tons of the stuff in 1909 to 14,234,000 tons in 1955, reaching 36,114,000 tons in 2000.[18] A food which Sidney Mintz described as "a rarity in 1650, a luxury in 1750," and "a virtual necessity by 1850" thus became omnipresent by 1950, already creeping into prepackaged foods not before thought of as in need of added sweetness.[19]

The sheer existence of such mammoth heaps of calories and carbohydrates in itself reveals that whatever their ads claimed, the supermarkets and their various suppliers and media representatives were never simply offering volume sales in response to customer demand. They were also creating that demand. Their frequent suggestions that women spend more in "a bright, inviting and sanitary store," to quote one trade catalogue of 1938, were never mere observations of existing reality. They were also shaping that reality, performative gestures meant to hitch gender normativity to self-service's rescaling of food consumption.[20] This much, perhaps, is uncontentious. It is true that in any capitalist economy supply always supplies new demands for customers to demand. But it was especially true of the US food industry in the late 1930s. Ongoing pressure on prices, ongoing growth in food productivity, improved highway networks, improved refrigerated road and rail distribution systems, new fertilizers and pesticides, and the "revolution in power farming" occasioned not only by new sugarcane and combine harvesters but also by such gasoline tractors as the Fordson and the Farmall: the combined effect of these complex and interlocking nonhuman agents was first to grow more food and then to keep it fresh and move it around, ensuring that America continued producing its celebrated plenitude during a Depression era of joblessness and flatlining pay.[21] Feminized "volumetric" self-service, or what some urban Americans would come to know as the supermarket by the end of the 1930s, presented a canny response to the perils of oversupply, a breakthrough into new capacities to ensure this nonhuman plenty still had somewhere to go. As such the supermarket was far closer to the grain silo, the rail depot, or even the sewage treatment works than its commercial promoters would ever admit. It was only a more "human" equivalent to such industrial way stations, another link in the chain that allowed wave after wave of American plant life to flow from seedling and soil extraction to factory before being returned to the biosphere in the form of treated human waste.

But it also becomes apparent that the supermarket could only join this "nonhuman" cycle if it reintroduced ideas of individuation associated with the human. Human fuel and fuel emissions then and now—what we call crops or food or shit depending on where it sits on the food cycle—usually travels around in big blocks. It is huddled into vast fields, silos, industrial livestock farms, and road and rail warehouses, and as it is funneled through underground pipelines during its final stages, it coagulates into undifferentiated blobs of matter in the posthuman soup of sewage basins. The minor miracle of an individual seedling in the field or embryo on the farm passes unnoticed and is accepted as one of a thousand or more only if it matches them in shape and size.[22] Yet into this system, designed to amalgamate food into homogenous mobile blocks, 1930s supermarkets reintroduced individuation at the level of customer choice. Anyone could see that unlike the main-street grocers they wanted to outcompete, such stores were first and foremost warehouses, way stations in a chain designed to carry food from its point of production to its point of disposal. Just like every other link in the chain, their main purpose was to optimize flow: to store and move food on to its next phase and thus to tailor what has since become known as "just in time," or JIT, distribution to food's various biological schedules of production and decay.[23] From their earliest origins, indeed, supermarkets pursued new forms of vertical integration, using their mounting dominance over the grocery sector to lock suppliers into exclusive and often unlucrative deals.[24] But at the same time, many of these stores went to increasing lengths to mask their commitment to optimal flow, taking pains to assure customers that they remained at the heart of the operation. Only a few emulated the rather disarming honesty Michael Cullen displayed when he told the New York press that King Kullen planned to open a dozen more "monstrous stores" and to "pile it high and sell it cheap" inside each one. Even those supermarkets which attached similar emphasis to "rock-bottom" prices often proved reluctant to link these discounts to the fact that their business model required customers to lift and transport their choices unassisted. Whereas Cullen was happy to allow his stores a utilitarian look, relying on curbside parking and presenting his discount goods "as if they lay in storage," many of his competitors distanced themselves from such "eastern monstrosity markets" (the phrase came from *Progressive Grocer* magazine) and continued to cater to their clientele's expectation of an aestheticized, convenient shopping experience.[25] Through soft electric lighting and tilted, geometric stock displays they endeavored to orient themselves around their individual customer, recasting the barnlike scale of their stores as "a housewife's paradise," her own "palace ... of plenty," and a manifestation less of nonhuman logistics than of a desire to honor her with a variety of fresh goods far wider than any she might find downtown.[26]

In the grocery sector of the late 1930s, then, the nonhuman imperatives of food flow were brought into a delicate balance with the rhetoric and practice of consumer choice. The new supermarket always served two masters, adjusting JIT dictates to food's varied schedules of decay even as it continued assuring its individuated human customers that it was delivering a cornucopian plenty made just for them. From afar you might have been forgiven for thinking that the food on the shelves of the new supermarket remained intact and in big blocks. On closer inspection, however, it would become clear that these big blocks, of course, were already divided, precut into easy 3-D jigsaws of multicolored boxes and bottles which now invited their permanent division and dispatch into a thousand private homes. Other features confirmed the existence of this unusual marriage of optimal flow and individual choice on the floor of the 1930s supermarket. Clothing, luxury, or less functional main-street stores often tried to hold their customers captive, capturing their attention through a canny sequence of window displays, airy stock layout, and face-to-face service. New supermarkets, on the other hand, often seemed quite happy to let their customers go home. In ad after ad they made common cause with the time-poor housewife, promising her easy parking and uncongested checkouts, or what *Progressive Grocer* editor Carl Dipman called "less waiting," "greater rapidity," and the prospect of shopping in an unbroken flow over smooth "linoleum" floors.[27] Yet while they thus established a clear synchronicity between human customers and nonhuman goods, ushering both toward the exit doors in the name of faster turnover, such efficiencies stood at an odd angle to the distracting gondola displays and the need "to keep changing ... floor displays," among the other methods by which the first supermarkets effectively revived the efforts at captivation or delay practiced by those downtown operations they were meant to be superseding. Saunders's aforementioned retreat from raw efficiency—his discovery that if he lifted his initial ban on backward steps and allowed his customers to shop slowly, "fine ideas for dishes and menus [would] keep bobbing up" in their minds—thus reverberated in many of the discussions that took place within the industry during the 1930s and 1940s. It found echoes not only as Dipman's *The Modern Grocery Store* advocated distracting island displays, for example, but also as he urged new businesses to adopt all manner of other "little stunts" to lure their customers into more circuitous routes around as many of their open shelves as possible.[28] No contemporary outfit sought to reintroduce the ultraefficient flows which Saunders had prescribed for his earliest branch stores of Piggly Wiggly. Most instead followed or intuited *The Modern Grocery Store*'s advice: the best and quickest way to shift your stock was actually to allow customers to delay—to all but encourage them to pause, reconsider, even retrace their steps, and no matter that the supermarket was meant to allow "merchandise to flow through at the least possible expense."[29] Ongoing debates today about the virtues of online shopping as well as the relative advantages of "clockwise" and "counterclockwise" floor plans often hinge on a similar tension between the commercial rhetoric of speed and the supermarket's less public knowledge that slowness and distraction often hold the key to higher sales.[30]

And so what also becomes apparent is that as the supermarket pushed the imperatives of optimal flow and consumer choice into this uneasy, fragile alliance, a new and distinctive way of shopping was born. Optimal flow and consumer choice, after all, pull in opposite directions. The first always seeks acceleration while the second, with its constant desire to distract, always wants to slow things down. The combination of these opposing forces in the supermarket could only cause confusion. For the new and emerging supermarkets were seeking, on the one hand, to harness the haptic encounter which brought Caroline Meeber to a complete standstill in The Fair. But their pursuit of faster turnover, on the other hand, left them even more determined to keep pulling shoppers toward the exit. A store which promised to do away with the haggling of the old city market and the scrutiny of the Victorian store thus now harassed its customers at a subtler and ontological level. Under its roof time kept moving two ways at once, always seeking to distract you but never quite letting you stop.

In Dreiser's novel, Carrie, lost in a world of luxury, shrinks from her desire, afraid her body will do damage to the "dainty" and "delicate" fripperies before her. There is a furtiveness to the scene—a sense that when placed before such open displays of luxury goods, even customers less aspirational than Carrie might start to fantasize about shoplifting. All the while Dreiser allows his own comments to intrude, suspending narrative time, or stretching it at least, and leaving us in no doubt that we are in the presence of a prophecy of some kind. But it is clear that as early as 1930, events were already racing ahead of that literary vision. *The Modern Grocery Store* again said it best. Flatly insisting that "the American grocery buyer is the American housewife," this business manual urged its readers to "take into account her peculiarities, her whims and fancies. We must remember that her senses are keenly developed—that she loves to browse about tempting foods—that she is happiest in the grocery store that surrounds her with merchandise in which she is interested and displays it well."[31] In urging proprietors to jettison all glass barriers, to fill their stores with open and "attractive displays," and to invite their shoppers to "wait on themselves," *The Modern Grocery Store* and other industry advisers in effect took *Sister Carrie*'s singular commodity experience, dislodged it from its original situation of luxury, and turned it into a rapid everyday encounter.[32] In the process, as they placed haptic susceptibility at the service of food flow, they also began to undermine their own gender assumptions. Even as they built their businesses around the belief that all women were impulsive and superficial, as open to suggestion as Carrie Meeber, they increasingly put these delicate creatures to work. For the phrase "wait on themselves" was of course euphemistic. Hidden behind it was the fact that the supermarket was now asking customers to perform much of the work of grocery shopping for themselves.

Via such contradictions self-service arrived at its unforeseen zenith; not because it offered new freedoms or variety, but because, as if against its own belief in pristine femininity, it enlisted women's hands and bodies in the frenetic work of grocery shopping. It placed before them a new way of shopping, asked them to go and grab their own goods all around the giant store, and at once encouraged and discouraged them from pausing or lingering as they did so. Gone now was Carrie's hesitation, her slow creeping up on The Fair's magic objects. By 1937 or 1938, while newspaper ads reverted to a familiar scenario (white woman, A-line skirt, empty basket, gloved hand, standing still, baring her teeth at the boxes on the shelf), the actual environments of actual stores were requiring such women's real-life counterparts (and lots of other customers too) to remain in motion—to be quick as they reached and grabbed, always pushing homeward in a new mode of shopping altogether "unladylike." In the real world, of course, only children or the clinically insane would ever smile back at the cartoon animals and racist "spokesservants" that beamed out at them from shelves that reached from above their heads right down to their feet. But even if other customers had wanted to follow suit, there was never enough time or space for them to do so. People behind them would get annoyed, and the sheer acreage of the supermarket meant that, in any case, they had to keep moving. Able to bypass only one or two of its aisles, they had to keep processing its wave of information, scanning left and right as they kept all their financial and family obligations in mind. They had to focus on the task in hand, fighting their way through to secure their personal bit of plenty from the store's towering walls of food.

CHAPTER FOUR

The Late Cart

As all these different features of the 1930s supermarket become apparent, bringing into view a new and uneasy marriage between individual choice and JIT flow, they also reveal an obvious omission.

Many of the other major developments that the supermarket sector introduced over the decade were proactive, pioneering new functions that customers had neither anticipated nor demanded. Hussmann, when launching its first open freezer cabinet in 1935, also needed to persuade its business clientele that a rise in sales would occur if they allowed their customers to reach in and select frozen foods for themselves. Customers themselves had not been lobbying for such a right.[1] Lower electricity costs, the improved safety and affordability of refrigeration technology, and the success of self-service display in a range of less chilly contexts instead persuaded the firm to abandon fridge doors altogether and make it even easier for shoppers to scoop up their own colorful cardboard boxes of Birdseye spinach, fish fillets, and Eskimo Fudge Pie.[2] Similarly, when the Package Machinery Company began to sing the praises of "printed cellophane" in the same period, the illustrations and explanations of its industry ads in effect conceded that its new product would not empower customers but tempt them into a less rational approach to food shopping. The arrival of see-through wrapping on the grocery shelves, it explained, would "enable" the "buyer to *see* the candy" among other enticing foods, generating an "*appetite appeal*" that would be immediate and lead to a flurry of almost unconscious "impulse" purchasing.[3]

But in 1936, when Sylvan N. Goldman and his employee Fred W. Young started playing around with castors, baskets, and folding chairs in Goldman's head office in Oklahoma City, they aimed neither to conjure new desires nor tap into latent impulses. They were addressing a problem long apparent for all to see. As we have seen, the debt that the new self-service enterprises owed to the highway networks was already apparent in the directional arrows and "continuous circuitous path" that Clarence Saunders had envisioned in 1917. But car culture, twenty years later, still met a limit inside every modern store. Customers, ever likelier to drive to a single supermarket for their own groceries, on arrival remained reliant on the "market baskets" also stipulated in Saunders's patent. And "women" in particular, Goldman had noticed, continued to exhibit "a tendency to stop shopping when" these "baskets became too full or heavy."[4] A simple limit in the physical strength of all his customers continued to impose a simple limit on the goods they could buy on a visit to one of his Standard or Humpty Dumpty stores.

Goldman had already tried to lighten these loads by other means. In his largest branch store of Standard earlier in the decade he had ordered several of his employees to walk around looking for any customers who appeared to be struggling with their groceries; the idea was to hand them an empty basket before ferrying their existing choices to the checkout.[5] But this measure soon proved unpopular, and added wage costs to a self-service business model supposedly based on removing clerks from the shop floor. As his supermarkets grew ever bigger—as early as 1925 they met *Fitch's* 1940 requirement that floor space in such stores exceed five thousand square feet—the problem before Goldman grew ever more pressing.[6] Unlike Saunders and many rivals in the industry, Goldman decided against scaling back or scrapping his stores' home delivery service. Unlike Cullen, he was happy to take the lead in the growing national trend of giving grocery store customers dedicated parking in adjacent lots.[7] Little could thus distract him from the simple problem created by all the beckoning signs, open shelves and fridges, and see-through packaging that he and his suppliers had arrayed around his store. His focus was on fixing the sheer immobilization that could occur if his shoppers succumbed as he hoped they would to all these bright and grabbable temptations.

Of course, in comparison to other developments of the time—the 1930s also witnessed the invention of jet aeronautics, the building of the Hoover Dam and Empire State Building, and the establishment of a new national highway network—this was a simple problem, far removed from the glories of the "American technological sublime."[8] It was not even all that new. Texas grocery chain Weingarten's had spotted it as early as the 1910s and had provided wheeled carriers on which customers could place their familiar "market" baskets and push them around—though hardly anyone did.[9] And despite this early failure, the central problem Weingarten's had addressed only deepened over the subsequent years. The mechanics of consuming plenty advanced apace over the next quarter century. Economic historian Alexander J. Field has argued that the 1930s were "the most technologically progressive decade of the century."[10] John Steinbeck's recollection that the fish canneries of Monterey, California, remained "rich and expanding" even amid the worst hardships of the Depression was, for Field, far from atypical.[11] A time of joblessness and hunger, the 1930s were also, Field notes, a decade in which truck registrations almost doubled, domestic fridge ownership rose sharply, and even the manufacturing of new cars, the majority of which now featured generous storage compartments, remained fairly steady.[12] Alongside acute economic despair, then, this was also the moment of possibility that Lewis Mumford captured in his *The Culture of Cities* (1938), a moment caught between a "Neotechnic" economy that had achieved "perfection" and "automatism in all machinery" and a fast-approaching "Biotechnic" world in which "the airplane, the phonograph, the motion picture, and modern contraception" would soon become familiar features of American life.[13] But inside the supermarket—at the epicenter of an emergent suburban future which *The Culture of Cities* could already see growing too insular and reliant on the car—shoppers remained stuck in the Stone Age. Surrounded by backlit electric signs, chrome fridges, and other Neotechnic gadgetry, they could only use the basic receptacle the store supplied, unable even to access the wheel-and-axle technology which Mumford had recently attributed to the "woodman" of Bronze Age Europe's "north coastal area."[14]

In Oklahoma City in the late 1930s, then, Goldman and Young were seeking a simple solution to a simple and long-standing problem. Their first attempt at this solution still looked like what it was—a simple basket on a folding chair on wheels. But it worked, and it did so because of some ingenious modifications. Alongside the wheels that they strapped to its feet, Goldman

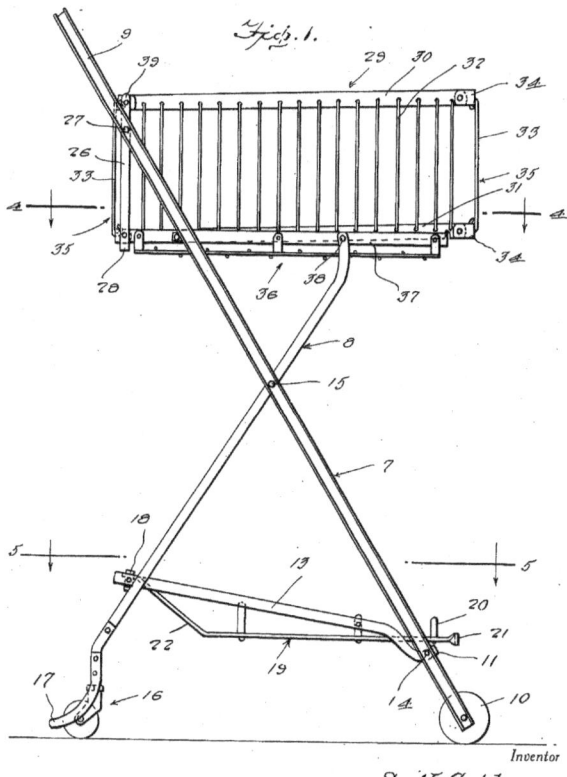

Figure 8. "Patent for *Combination Basket and Carriage*," 4 May 1937, Sylvan N. Goldman.

and Young also added a rack for a lower basket, recast its backrest as a handlebar, and retained its folding mechanism as a way of saving on storage space. What resulted was clearly basic, even primitive in design. But largely thanks to Young's extensive technical experience—in July 1935 this man whom others dismissed as Goldman's "carpenter" had filed a patent of his own for a folding shopping basket—it was already a useful and usable invention.[15] As Goldman's patent of May 1937 confirms, it already incorporated front castors which swiveled left and right, allowing it to turn from aisle to aisle. The combined leverage of its four wheels, meanwhile, ensured that any customer who chose to place a second "ordinary market basket" onto "the rack at the bottom" could still push it around with ease.[16]

Certain technical problems remained. As Grandclément notes, the prototype "tended to return to the state of a chair and to fold up when the wheels bumped into something," and its high center of gravity left it prone "to tip over when going round corners."[17] But Young's background in innovation again helped him, over months of trial and error, to rectify these technical defects. His know-how was crucial in allowing Goldman to file a second patent in March 1938 for a cart that now featured a "dependable structural assemblage" and a new "toggle joint action" which afforded improved "rigidity when the structure is erected so that it is virtually locked in open position and not likely to accidentally collapse."[18] In collaboration, and despite the existence of clear precedents and rivals, Goldman and Young thus took a decisive step toward the production and popularization of a "volumetric" indoor cart that would in time lead to all the 2-D and 3-D carts now so ubiquitous around the world. A contraption which Goldman first patented as a "novel rollable market basket carriage" but which he would in time learn to call a "supermarket cart" clearly provided the new and industrial system of food supply with what Grandclément has called the "last link in the ... chain."[19] And yet, of all these links, and notwithstanding Young's ingenuity, it was also far and away the simplest. It was unfuelled; it relied on unpowered wheels. It was primitive; in Mumford's historical schemata, it belonged at most to the "Eotechnic," or Neolithic, phase. It could never really rival the new harvesting and refrigeration technologies which had called it into existence.

But still, and even though its mechanical advantages were so clear, customers continued to resist it. Often, upon introducing the other elements (or Latourian "plug-ins") which have since become commonplace in supermarkets around the world, the new American grocery stores of the 1930s worked hard to guide their customers, helping them to remain "locally and provisionally competent" by posting friendly instructions and even including explanations in local newspaper ads. Cereal boxes and other goods were far from the only nonhuman agents that addressed shoppers as they toured the supermarket's aisles. Miscellaneous in-store commands did too. Etched in cursive or Disneyesque fonts, signs above self-service fridges invited them to "Reach in!" and "Serve Yourself!" and the appearance of toiletries or other new stock lines was often accompanied by posters exhorting passersby to "Look what this counter does!"[20] Left up for too long and often too obvious for words, such signs would soon become the stuff of postwar nightmares; they are heard "shouting" from the "chromium shelves" in Shirley Jackson's *Hangsaman* (1951), while Allen Ginsberg would parody their overinsistent exclamations in his comic journey around the supermarket ("Wives in the avocados! Babies in the tomatoes!").[21] But whereas these aggressive, bossily helpful signs could prove too ubiquitous in other contexts, the evidence suggests that when planning to launch his first batch of carts in the summer of 1937, Goldman avoided them altogether. Instead he took a more measured approach. Planning a quiet launch for his invention, he placed an ad in the *Oklahoma City Times,* using it to ask a cryptic question:

> Can you imagine wending your way through a spacious food market without having to carry a cumbersome shopping basket on your arm? That's what you'll find at the Standard. Just pick your items from the shelves. They will be checked and placed in your car without having to carry a single item. The Standard shopping way is a revelation in food buying and every customer who visits our stores this week end will see the latest device conceived by the mind of man: and be able to shop with an ease never before known in any Food Store.[22]

The ad, as Grandclément comments, was a kind of tease. It promised unnamed freedoms, even suggesting a magic suspension of gravity, but it offered no "information as to how this miracle would occur." Readers could only discover the solution to the "riddle" if they agreed to turn themselves "into customers and to visit Goldman's shops, where a hostess offered them" replicas of the basket carrier he and Young had devised. Yet, as Grandclément adds, launching his carts in such an indirect manner soon proved something of a mistake. Some of the men among his clientele "protested that they were strong enough to carry baskets themselves," while "the women argued that they had pushed around enough baby carriages in their lives not to want the same yoke in the grocer store. Only the elderly customers used them."[23] That dislike of the cart which has been such a mainstay of its history, a factor not only in its delayed invention but also in ongoing efforts to replace it, thus seems apparent in its first appearance on the US supermarket scene. At first, and for one reason or another, grocery customers who had accepted several startling developments over the 1930s, from the vanishing of shop floor staff to the introduction of prepackaged meats, proved reluctant to embrace a simple machine whose only purpose was to ease their movement through the store. Even though Goldman's flagship supermarket in Oklahoma City now appeared to demand such mechanical assistance—by this time it had grown to seven thousand square feet, with a parking lot twice this size—his customers still clung to the "cumbersome," preferring regulation baskets intended to serve the smaller stores of generations past.[24]

Different stories exist about what Goldman did next. In one of the earliest renditions, in Max Zimmerman's *The Super Market: A Revolution in Distribution* (1955), Goldman hired a group of "attractive girls" to act as in-store demonstrators. This version of events, however, might tell us more about Zimmerman's imagination or the objectifying reflexes of the 1950s than what really happened. Other, more reliable accounts suggest that Goldman went to some lengths to select a cast that resembled the demographic range of his "typical" customers as far as possible. Eager to show that his new carts "weren't wheeled monsters," he gave to this group of "ordinary" Oklahomans a simple and easy job.[25] He asked them to take a "monster" each, to push it up and down his store, and to fill it up with groceries, thus showing everyone around them exactly how to shop now that the age of the supermarket cart had dawned.[26] The ruse worked. Quickly, and whether or not they knew they had been privy to his secret drama, Goldman's customers followed the example of these demonstrators, overcoming any initial aversion to the cart that they had felt. Soon afterward they could be seen pushing his simple yet somehow patented machines all around his oversized stores. And soon after that his workers no longer even needed to remind these customers to fill both baskets. A more pressing concern was the fact that they had started placing their children in the lower of the two.

As orders started flowing in—first from a chain in Amarillo, Texas, and then from further afield—such considerations soon acquired public currency.[27] In August 1940, just three years after Goldman and Young finished experimenting in Oklahoma City, an issue of the *Saturday Evening Post* dedicated to the "Colossal Supermarket" could already confirm the new national familiarity of their double-decker cart. "Lunchtime at the Grocery," the cover illustration Albert W. Hampson provided for the magazine, centers on a reproduction of this contraption so faithful that it even depicts Goldman's patented specification of fixed wheels at the rear and swiveling castors at the front. In producing his picture, however, Hampson also took care to air the new anxieties suggested in his satirical title. Into his cart's lower basket he has placed a small white boy who eats a banana with one hand while delving into a barrelful of sweets with the other. The cart thus already casts something of a spell over him, piloting him toward a range of "Serve Yourself" signs and snacks he cannot resist. As such Hampson's illustration, in recognizing the cart as a new and commonplace object of American life, also implicates it in a new identity and holds it responsible for the emergence of a "child consumer" in whom childishness and choice are perilously entwined. Indeed, while some scholars today question many of the assumptions behind subsequent postwar complaints about "pester power," Hampson's sarcastic title alone makes clear that, for him, the child and the consumer which form the two elements in this new identity exist in contradiction.[28] It certainly seems unlikely that his boy, his body already a little chubby, will soon get any smaller.

A certain ambivalence thus always shadowed the shopping cart's gradual colonization of the foodscapes of the United States. Even customers who had long been lugging their groceries around the supermarket often saw this simple contraption as another burden, or "yoke," rather than a labor-saving device. For many years, as Franck Cochoy has observed, even the leading trade magazine *Progressive Grocer* "did not really know what to say about" carts, a silence Cochoy attributes to the fact that they were "the grocer's property but also the customer's tool" and hence a "boundary object... between human and non-human agencies."[29] For supermarket patrons and promoters alike, then, the cart remained uncomfortable but useful, a simple machine that was required by a system that it threatened to reveal as an otherwise industrial, nonhuman food chain. Yet the sheer usefulness of the cart has always eclipsed such negative connotations. By the end of the 1930s Goldman went from success to success, imposing his patent on rival manufacturers and receiving more orders for his Folding Cart Company than he could keep up with. Although little fanfare accompanied the proliferation of his product, it proliferated nonetheless. As Grandclément remarks:

> On a national scale the story of the diffusion of the folding cart is much the same. Nationally, the customers were not the end users but the managers of supermarkets. Goldman took advantage of the first Super Market Convention in September 1937 to launch his product and said that he received favorable appreciations from supermarket operators. But when Goldman's sales representative went to visit supermarket's managers, he encountered terrible resistances. They were worried about the damage that their

customers' children could cause by playing with shopping carts, for instance, and consequently refused to buy Goldman's carts. Goldman then used his employees as actors to make a movie showing the perfect order with which stores equipped with carts functioned. Pleased and reassured by what they saw, supermarket managers ended up adopting Goldman's folding cart. That was how the folding cart invaded the world of mass consumption and Goldman's new firm, the Folding Basket Carrier Corporation, was outstandingly prosperous.[30]

In the work of Bruno Latour, as James Mussell has argued, the notion of invention "involves a complex process in which a new thing is allocated a moment of discovery while" it is "simultaneously granted a constant (but hidden) presence throughout all time."[31] Such an "allocation," in the case of the supermarket, has to some always seemed difficult to achieve. Even in the postwar years, when its conquering of the grocery sector remained a major source of media debate, important observers such as Milton Friedman already believed that this new kind of store was "unpatentable" in general, and too much of a mishmash of known or obvious innovations for any individual entrepreneur to "allocate" a single moment "of discovery" within it.[32]

This, though, was never Goldman's view. Instead he followed Clarence Saunders's example. In his first submission, as we have seen, Saunders presented himself as the creator of a "self-serving store," framing his patent in a vocabulary of innovation. But a closer inspection of these descriptions also confirms that they speak of *newness* or *invention* only when they are explaining some of the specific and indeed quite eccentric details of Saunders's store design. On the other hand, whenever his patent refers to its central title, Saunders drops his talk of innovation and speaks instead of the "improvements" he is making to such stores, thereby admitting in effect that they already existed.³³ And yet it would not be long before official plaques and other monuments would hail Piggly Wiggly's first store in Memphis the "first self-service" business of all, overwriting Saunders's own semantic distinctions to "allocate" to him what really remained quite undefinable and diffuse, a cultural phenomenon more than an invention per se.³⁴ The folding cart patents that Goldman filed in 1936 and 1937 instigated a similar pattern. Necessarily, these too labored over quite particular, even idiosyncratic, details; Goldman could hardly lay claim to a basic structure that peasant laborers remained reliant on throughout the world. But this was another distinction that soon got lost in the mix. As if overnight, in the mysterious questions he published in the *Oklahoma City Times* in 1937, Goldman was already promising a "revelation" and "the latest device conceived by the mind of man," his hyperbole racing ahead of the particularities of his patents. "Years later," as Grandclément notes, the contribution that Goldman would allow to be "allocated" to himself—Oklahoman benefactor, patron of the arts, inventor of the supermarket cart—would seem "really different," bearing little relationship to its original basis in the new "toggle joint action" and "dependable structural assemblage" which he had originally drawn to the attention of the Patent Office.³⁵ The annals of popular US history, always looking out for heroes, thus found an eager volunteer in Goldman. While his "allocation" as the inventor of the shopping cart has probably gained wider public acceptance than Saunders's "allocation" as the inventor of self-service, both men took great lengths to claim "inventions" that actually combined existing solutions for new commercial ends.

    There is little doubt that Goldman worked hard to bring this distillation about. Certainly, even if they never remotely delivered the technological wizardry that his ads promised, his and Young's patented designs always identified practical problems and provided easy solutions to them. The title of a later patent, filed by Young as Goldman's assignee, nicely captured his variety of entrepreneurial genius. *Folding Baby Seats for Nesting Carriers* was indeed a safe and integrated child seat, a design which allowed the child to face "the customer ... with its lower extremities extending out through openings formed in the gate," and which remains, with only minor modifications, in widespread use all around the world today.[36] As such, alongside his central claim to the cart itself, Goldman was also quick to grasp that when they placed their children into the lower basket of his design, his customers brought along another pair of eyes, and another set of hunger pangs, to their regular supermarket visits. Supermarkets clearly did need to be concerned about the fact that so many of their customers were squeezing their children into the lower basket of his original patented design. But Goldman recognized that this represented an opportunity as much as a danger, and seized it with a modification that allowed children, with their love of sugar and all things suboptimal, to tour the enticing aisles. The child seat patents Goldman filed after the war confirmed his approval of a phenomenon which his first designs had, perhaps by accident, instigated.

But nor is there much doubt that Goldman was an opportunist, quick to claim credit for innovations already in use. Weingarten's unsuccessful "basket carriers" of the 1910s amounted to an uncomfortable precedent for Goldman's efforts to cast himself as the sole inventor of the cart, and his *Collapsing Seat for Nesting Carriers* only formalized his customers' existing habit of turning Standard/Humpty Dumpty's carts into makeshift child seats. Quick on his feet, Goldman's opportunism largely served him well. His Folding Carrier Company made him a millionaire, and before his death in 1984 he enjoyed the lavish praise of Terry Wilson's hagiographic *The Cart That Changed the World: The Career of Sylvan N. Goldman* (1978). But it could also lead him into difficulties, and never more so than in that telltale word *Nesting*, which in itself suggests that his postwar patents offered adaptations for new forms on the market that other innovators had developed. The invention of the cart was, in other words, always a collaborative venture, begun by Weingarten and unknown others and continued by a range of innovators through the twentieth century rather than just Goldman or, indeed, Young. Of all these other innovators by far the most important was Orla E. Watson. As Grandclément notes, "alterations" Watson made to "the shopping cart" in the months after World War Two

> warrant particular attention, as with hindsight they seem so obvious and simple that their significance could easily be underestimated. The 1946 telescoping carts differed from their predecessors in two ways. They not only fitted into one another, owing to the swinging gate at the rear end of the baskets, but were also attached to the baskets so that they were permanently *shopping carts* and no longer basket carriers with distinct, separable elements.... From the self-service development logic, this simplification is particularly interesting insofar as it allows for a transfer of the effort of putting the cart into use from the store employees to the customers. This, in addition, permits a quasi-perfect adjustment of the rate of stock-flow conversion to the customers' flows. Thus, both the availability of shopping carts and storage space are not only increased but permanently optimized.[37]

Among a few misgivings that Graham Harman has expressed about the work of his fellow philosopher Bruno Latour, perhaps the most important hinges on Latour's emphasis on the autonomy of process. "Undeserving losers," Harman suggests, often risk being overlooked in his philosophical system.[38] Their forgotten inventions can come to appear a kind of failed "alliance," and this failure can in turn be put down to the human agent's incomprehension of his or her negotiation of a given nonhuman force. By extension, even a clear innovation like Watson's can come to seem inevitable or latent in the agency of the object itself, as though the invention always wanted to be invented and the inventor had only helped it along. The focus of Grandclément's account can help us to avoid this risk. Its sheer detail can help us "reallocate" an innovation to a single innovator who is often overlooked even in the modest context of the cart's humdrum global odyssey. Thanks to it we can now recognize that Orla E. Watson invented one of the smallest but most abiding features of the modern shopping cart. He alone placed a "swinging gate" at its rear end and thus created its nesting function. He alone allowed us to end our shopping expedition with a simple assault, throwing our cart with an angry clatter into an empty waiting row.

By the end of the 1950s the commuters of Long Island were well accustomed to living in the suburbs. They already inhabited what Christopher Wells calls "Car Country," the new "monoculture" of private residences, vanishing sidewalks, and a dependency on the car so acute they needed to "reach ... for the car keys" just to post a letter or get to school.[39] Like billions around the world today, however, many Long Islanders in the late 1950s had also already discovered that the cars which were proving so useful for shopping and leisure activities were all but useless for traveling to work. Congestion and the forbidding expense of parking in Manhattan meant that when many reached for their

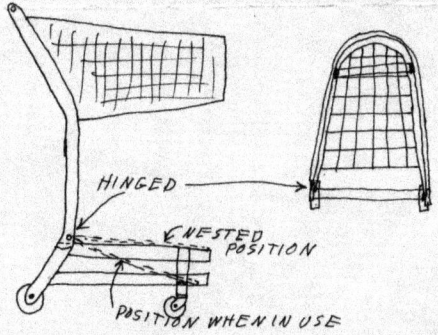

Figure 9. "Telescope Cart Drawing on Letterhead," 1946, Orla E. Watson.

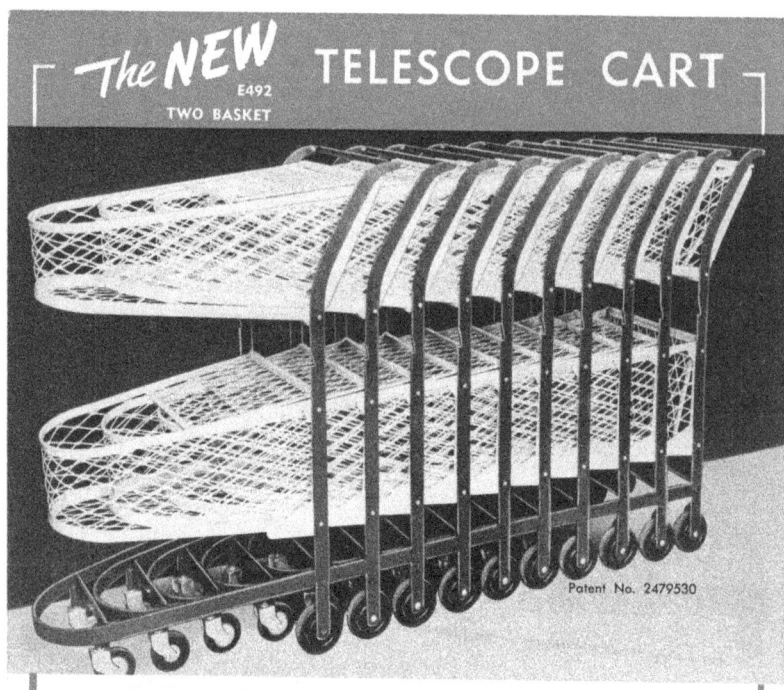

Figure 10. "The New Telescope Cart," ad, 1949, Orla E. Watson.

keys on weekday mornings, they did so to drive just a short distance, parking in the nearest station of the Long Island Rail Road (or LIRR). On arrival, key in pocket, they swapped their private cars for a communal train—and they stepped back into an environment which had been designed and built in the early 1930s, and which had been struggling to compete for the public funding lavished upon the state's highways ever since. The consequences on board, as recollected by Robert A. Caro in 1973, were predictable:

> Getting a seat was not total victory. Getting an end seat was what counted. Many of the LIRR seats had been designed for three people—but they had been designed half a century before, when people were smaller. There wasn't enough room for three people. Sitting in even an end seat was indignity; it was sitting with your shoulder and thigh tight against a stranger's shoulder and thigh, pressing into him at every lurch, pushing against him while opening a newspaper or reaching into a pocket for your train ticket, surreptitiously taking advantage of shifts in his position to gain an extra quarter inch for your leg or arm. But sitting in the middle was indignity doubled.... It was no wonder that the first two persons to reach the three-man seats took the two end positions, and that when a third arrived, invariably the one sitting on the outside, closest to the aisle, would, instead of politely sliding over to make room for the new man on the outside, stand up and let him by to take the middle seat, careful not to look him in the eye.[40]

The history of the development of US industrial food production and distribution that has unfolded over the previous pages also casts a different light on this embarrassing vignette. In my brief account of the new and accelerated system of food flow that US innovation put in place in the middle of the twentieth century, the supermarket has perhaps emerged both as just another link in the chain and as a point of sudden differentiation—a place which mastered the art of taking this industry's vast slabs of food, splitting them into tiny identical units, and putting these in easy reach of millions of shoppers. And the cart has perhaps emerged, in turn, as the perfect instrument of this sudden differentiation, as an instrument whose open steel cage allowed such shoppers to delve for themselves into these walls of plenty, and whose castors urged them to do so quickly, aiding turnover as it ushered them home without delay. If the supermarket's vocation was thus to allow nonhuman food to flow into human homes, then the cart's masterstroke was to hand this complex differentiation to the occupants of those homes, persuading them to carry out processes which had before fallen to shop staff.

Of course, all this might only confirm an ambivalence many of us already felt, and might only lead us to view the supermarket and the supermarket cart with a renewed sense of cynical or fatalistic awe. The scale of the supermarket here certainly remains impressive. The shopping system that men such as Saunders, Cullen, and Goldman brought to completion (for customers they imagined as female and white) now seems not just efficient and epic but ingenious, and not least because of Goldman's final popularization of a cart which clicked into place like a battery in a watch, helping food flow down all sorts of new and individuated routes. Certainly, without Goldman's entrepreneurialism, it is hard to see how Walmart could later have gained such total control over global supply and distribution, or amassed a fortune now equal to the combined wealth of the thirty-five million poorest US families.[41] Nor would Fredric Jameson have found in the Arkansan supermarket a curious "utopian" potential, or revolutionary capacity, which it could unleash if only it acted in "exactly the opposite way," channeling its energies no longer toward profit but to improving life for customers and suppliers alike.[42] But to recognize the power of the supermarket is also to become skeptical of its own incessant rhetoric of convenience and choice. It is to realize, first, that the supermarket could only bring the industrial food chain to completion once its leading pioneers had grasped that (in contrast to all their talk of variety and ease) the human needs that they were feeding were in fact predictable and that the materials which satisfied them could be bundled into large and moveable blocks. And it is to realize, second, that all the supermarket's promises of convenience—all the gimmicks, devices, and ploys by which it claimed to make life easier for its customers—only addressed a problem of its own devising, easing a task of food distribution it had handed to its own shoppers.

Customers, in the rhetoric of the supermarket, are always central, and every new policy or procedure it adopts always seeks to capture them both for now and for the future. But the supermarket in practice has split loyalties and pays equal attention to the biological lifespans and climatic requirements of its nonhuman stock. Any equivalization of nonhuman carts and human stomachs, in the sphere of supermarket marketing, is out of the question: every customer is unique, awash with individual desires, and the cart only helps to satisfy them. And in general, through its endless campaigns against mold and bacteria and irregular plant and animal life, the supermarket works hard to uphold that boundary between "inside" and "outside," which our metabolisms then complicate and even transcend.[43] And yet, if the aesthetic regime of supermarket hygiene thus sits oddly alongside the extravagant obliterations of our digestive enzymes, then in other spheres—and especially in the sphere of supermarket logistics—human stomachs and nonhuman carts are not antithetical at all. On the contrary, they rhyme. Both store food and transform its identity; both follow known and predictable routes; and both are crucial conduits in the differentiated, domestic stages of the industrial food chain.

Usually our vanity prevents us from recognizing this equivalence. On the Long Island commuter trains of the late 1950s, however, there were clearly moments not only of embarrassment but recognition, an apprehension that the human bodies of "car country" had outgrown the ergonomics of the industrial age. For the commuters who squashed themselves into the mass transit systems of the earlier social formation now really belonged to the new suburban world that waited for them on the other side of the tracks. They were habitués of optimal flow: of Robert Moses's Northern State Parkway and other sweeping road systems, and of the King Kullens and other supermarkets which had wasted no time chasing these highways deep into Long Island. And they were the product, too, of the "obesogenic" environment which the new "space-time feeling" of that car-based suburbia had brought about, and of all the beckoning roadside arrows and billboard ads and TV and radio jingles which urged them to indulge in what Graham Finlayson and Michelle Dalton have called the "repeated overconsumption" of "hyper-palatable ... foods ... high in fat and sugar."

Human differentiation, of course, continued amid this change; as Finlayson and Dalton recognize, "not all individuals have the same vulnerability to the" omnipresent "availability" of "hyper-palatable food."[44] But Caro's observations make clear that by 1960 the size of these suburban bodies had expanded on average and overall, and statistics confirm that they would soon grow bigger still.[45] Variant, differentiated human physique, taken overall, thus followed the example of standardized nonhuman cavities in the age of increased capacity. People in the suburbs grew in step with the larder fridges in their kitchens and the storage compartments at the rear of their cars, and some grew as big as the carts they pushed around their local stores.[46] The stories of John Cheever often invite us to picture these expanded Americans, crammed into hot and humid carriages of the kind Caro describes, and longing to return to their modern cars and the smooth cloverleaf junctions and drive-thrus and supermarkets that would allow them to grow bigger still. Indeed, in Cheever's stories, trains, returning to suburban stations, can inspire a routine liberation: a "jackpot of humanity" spills onto the platform, and "numerous and eager" commuters walk joyously, "like sailors home from the sea," back to their parked cars.[47] Yet such suburban homecomings at the same time reveal the common and even endemic nature of the physical enlargement. Some of Cheever's major characters are "still slender," "careful" about their "weight," and some of his minor characters are derided for letting themselves go. But his train scenes in general concur with Caro in the sense that they confirm that passengers were indeed getting larger en masse, and that any individual lapse into obesity, although still inviting hostile judgment, also reflected a structural or demographic drift. Our historic tendency to explain overeating in terms of individual failure or weakness consequently seems powerless to explain the more general expansion that Cheever implies and Caro conveys in terms of the unwelcome intimacies that happened aboard Long Island's rush-hour trains. For this was not greed or sin, and it was surely not a sign that a whole generation was lacking in restraint. It was instead a sign that this original group of New York commuters already inhabited a world like that of today, a world of cheap and suboptimal temptations, of gravity's private technological alleviations, of easy, secret excess—a world that made overconsumption seem natural and de rigueur. Even when these commuters were stuck in their ancient carriages, longing for their cars, the supermarket cart—Goldman's original "wheeled monster"—cast its spell.

CHAPTER FIVE

Carts Unchained

Soon thereafter, and at least from 1940 on, these "wheeled monsters" started rolling out—first to supermarket chains across the United States and then to all the country's major trading partners around the world. It was in these years that cart replicas complete with folding mechanisms and integrated child seats began to appear far beyond the reach of Watson's commercial interests or Goldman's patent lawyers. In 1953, three decades after Clarence Saunders had spoken of opening up a new Antipodean front for his Piggly Wiggly franchise, the Australian businessman M. A. T. Beshara returned from a research trip to the USA with news of the supermarket and installed a row of carts next to the entrance of a new store he opened in the new suburbs that were then starting to follow the Anzac Highway out of Adelaide to the coast.[1] In 1957, ahead of rival French firms Leclerc or Monoprix, the self-service chain Goulet-Turpin created a petite version of these carts and introduced them to customers at the new Express Marché that it opened in Paris west of the Bois de Boulogne.[2] Meanwhile, with its "automatic doors," "large stacks of fruit," and "caster-wheel carts [that] could move anywhere within the store," the 1950s setting of Satoshi Azuchi's *Supermarket* (1984) confirms that Japanese society in general had grown familiar with the practicalities of a supermarket approach which had been confined to Tokyo's Little America in the early stages of the Marshall Plan.[3] Whereas in the immediate aftermath of war the Japanese had "turned to the black market to survive" while US military personnel "shopped at PXs and commissaries filled to the brim with luxury items as well as hardy staples," the populace of Tokyo and other major centers soon afterward found they could carry out such shopping for themselves—and that they could enlist the cart to help them do it.[4]

But it is also clear that as these "monsters" spread throughout the world, placing a beckoning and "volumetric" void in front of grocery shoppers everywhere from Kyoto to Toulouse, they continued to escape rather than attract attention. The exception Goldman made for his carts in Oklahoma City—his decision to ignore the supermarket's usual array of advisory signs and to introduce his carts mysteriously and without direct explanation—found echoes on the Anzac Highway and off the Bois de Boulogne. Beyond American borders, too, the sudden appearance of boxes on wheels "just happened," being a minor and ignorable feature of this or that store's program of modernization. Customers here too would quickly accept such carts as a mechanism for gathering up their own differentiated portions of plenty, and as they did so their initial indifference toward these contraptions could give way to the ambivalence already captured on the American covers of *Life* and the *Saturday Evening Post.*

Following 1945, then, as many different countries fell under what Christopher Hitchens once called "the gravitational pull of planet America," the cart often seemed too basic to be numbered among the leading catalysts of this new international alignment. Unlike rock and roll, Hollywood, or other resonant US cultural forces, they caused no thrills, no dangerous sensations in their new international audiences. Unlike Coca Cola and Marlboro among other leading US brands, they usually seemed "unpatentable" and without genesis. Local firms around the world often approached their tubular handlebars as a blank space on to which they could paste logos and catchphrases already familiar to existing clienteles. And unlike Boeing airplanes and Zenith TVs among other leading US technological wonders, the imitation of these machines in the Communist bloc required no industrial espionage, insider knowledge, or specialist research teams. They never factored all that much in any of the calculations of US power which intensified as the Cold War took hold. Over the duration of that Cold War period, only a handful ever protested the introduction of such carts and fewer still ever welcomed them. But billions began to use them—and many did so at least once a week.

This way of overlooking the cart also extended to the famous visit that Nikita Khrushchev spent between the Atlantic and Pacific coasts during the early fall of 1959. Khrushchev's US hosts, of course, were at pains to ensure that after fourteen days in their country he would be left in no doubt about US technological prowess, and they ensured that by the time he returned to Moscow he had seen a good cross-section of its signal modern achievements: the airliners of Boeing, the skyscrapers of Manhattan, the concrete ribbons of Robert Moses's newest highways—and a branch store of Safeway in suburban San Francisco. Khrushchev drew crowds wherever he went in America, some friendly and some hostile, and the last of these visits proved to be no exception; the store's aisles were so full of onlookers there was no space for him or anyone to push a cart around. Even if room had permitted, however, it seems unlikely that Khrushchev or his hosts would have displayed anything like as much interest in these simple vehicles as they showed in the cavernous open freezers and backlit electric signage and shelves overflowing with the fruits of the late summer. "The image of the supermarket as a kind of pleasure palace took on special political significance in cold war rhetoric," as Tracey Deutsch has noted, but the government's hopes of making political capital out of the modern grocery store did not extend to its ubiquitous cart.[5] It was left to apparatchiks from his politburo, during far quieter and less publicized visits to the United States, to see the supermarket in action and even to meet and talk with its ordinary customers. Eight months before Khrushchev's visit to a cart-free Safeway, for example, his deputy premier Anastas Mikoyan took some time out from meetings on Capitol Hill and Embassy Row to see another side of Washington, DC. As *Le Monde* reported:

> During his visit to the "supermarket," Mr. Mikoyan stopped to watch an American housewife accompanied by her husband pushing her metal basket with wheels on which was sitting comfortably a baby of six months. Approaching the group, the First Vice-President of the Council of the USSR handed the baby a Russian candy, wrapped in paper decorated with a polar bear. Ravi, the child, got hold of it, and Mr. Mikoyan, smiling, shook hands with his stunned parents.
>
> In front of the meat counter Mr. Mikoyan took a plastic-wrapped steak and, leaning over Mr. Menshikov, murmured; "Is it for one person?" Mr. Mikoyan shook his head incredulously listening to the butcher boy's affirmative answer. "It seems to me to be a huge portion for one person," he said.

The Soviet leader stopped for a long time in front of the huge supermarket counter-fridge and further on he seemed very happy to find on the shelf of the preserves a jar of Russian "borscht" made in the USA.[6]

The exchange recalls Queen Elizabeth II's visit, less than two years earlier, to a branch store of Giant elsewhere in the city. As relayed by the *Saskatoon Star-Phoenix* and others at the time, Elizabeth and her husband Philip shared Mikoyan's curiosity in the store's shopping carts and the expectations and interactions of the people they found pushing them:

> Queen Elizabeth dropped unexpectedly into a supermarket at the peak of the Saturday afternoon rush and browsed around while several hundred suburban shoppers stood by, wide-eyed with amazement at the royal visit....
>
> "Ill just never get over this!," exclaimed ... Terry Moatz, as the Queen moved along after stopping to ask how often she shopped and to compliment her on her children.... The Queen stopped and chatted with several women shoppers and told Mrs. Fred Ricardi, with a youngster sitting in the baby seat atop her shopping cart, that "it's very nice to be able to bring your child here." ...
>
> Prince Philip stopped by Doc Hessler, a glazier, shopping with two youngsters, and asked how often he came out to buy the groceries. Hessler said once a week. The princed [*sic*] picked up the single cucumber at the bottom of Hessler's cart and quipped: "You haven't got very far, have you?" ...
>
> "How are you going to get all that home?" he asked a woman customer paying for several bags of groceries. She explained that she had her car parked outside the supermarket.[7]

Both encounters open a level beyond, or beneath, the geopolitical. Even as they hint at a certain theatricality, implying that the Soviet apparatchik and the British monarchs alike were playing up to their expected roles of unworldliness and wonder, their willingness to perform such parts has the effect of suspending questions of national comparison and establishing human encounters which seem more natural. The cart in turn proves central to this neutralization of ideological difference. Like cars or TVs, the electrified surrounds of the supermarket experience—the automatic doors, piped music, and vast illuminated fridges—could easily be taken as evidence that even after Yuri Gagarin made it into space in 1961, the future still belonged to the USA. Soviet leaders could either seek to emulate such new objects or deride them as sops to bourgeois individuality; like so much else at the time, they were magnetized by the pervading forces of Cold War competition. For Mikoyan, however, the sheer simplicity of "the metal basket with wheels" seems somehow to immunize it from such geopolitical considerations. He seems able to engage with it and indeed its young passenger on a simple and nonideological basis—on the same basis, perhaps, on which it could have been exhibited in Zagreb to Josip Tito in 1957 without causing concern about Yugoslavia's disposition toward the USA. Here again the sheer simplicity of the cart seemed to place it at an instinctive level "above" or "below" culture. Cleansed of ideology, the carts that soon began to appear in food stores in Leningrad and Moscow did not need to appear "American" or suspect. They could be lifted out of their original contexts and understood instead as a part of what the British novelist Francis Spufford has called the idea of *Red Plenty* (2012), the conveyances of an optimistic feeling that the Soviet Union, too, was now entering a moment of "cream and dumplings" when the work of the revolution "all paid off."[8]

But the feeling that the supermarket cart belonged to a world beyond ideology also formed a strange echo of the discreet and understated terms in which Goldman and Young had first introduced it to their customers in prewar Oklahoma. Goldman and Young, too, undertaking an intricate sequence of patented modifications, sought to create a cart that would be simple, duplicable, easy, and inconspicuous, while the crucial "telescoping" function that Orla E. Watson then added likewise ensured that it would be unobtrusive, too, and could sit waiting next to the entrance as customers rushed toward the electric and streamlined steel displays of the supermarket itself.[9] Nor was the cart the only element of the supermarket's foodscape that was designed to seem natural and to court an unconscious response. Packaging, too, often hid intricate processes of design from view, harnessing the cart's new capacities to join it in the realm of "impulse" or natural desires seemingly beyond ideology. Indeed, for the packaging maestro Walter Landor, the simplicity and the easy ergonomics of the supermarket cart presented a clear source of inspiration. The packaging and promotion company which Landor founded in San Francisco in 1941 stood out because of the careful attention it paid to the actual shopping contexts in which the boxes, jars, and bottles it produced would sit. As the architectural magazine *Forum* reported in 1962, Landor's headquarters were "a far cry from most workaday office interiors," and not least because their "conversion of an old pier on San Francisco's waterfront" included a "laboratory supermarket."[10] The journalist Dorothy Diamond confirmed that this "laboratory" was often filled with "men and women [who] propel carts through the aisles," doing so for "a fee and even babysitter expenses…. A research-design team observes their behaviour at gondolas and rack."[11] Landor himself took pride in the design, describing his company's approach to testing new commissions in lavish detail in *Food Field Reporter* and several other contemporary journals:

> The production is price-marked and displayed in the same facing and quantity ratio as in the average supermarket. Surrounding the client's product are the same competing products and other related items consumers have been led to expect. After the lab supermarket has been prepared, a group of consumers are invited in who have been carefully screened by a sociologist to represent a cross-section of the buying public. To assure a fresh viewpoint, none has served before or will ever serve again in a Landor project.... They are then given a supermarket cart, and asked to make a number of specific purchases.[12]

As early as 1948 Landor could already sound dismissive of his rivals. Other companies, he claimed, typically produced a packaging design that was pleasing or pretty but which just sat on supermarket shelves "silently... hoping some customer will notice it, recognize it as the product she'd seen advertised, and like it sufficiently to pick it up and give it a home." He drew a sharp distinction between these inert ornaments and the way his own vibrant items had already begun to "speak up" and "shout loudly" to the passing supermarket customer, imploring her to scoop them from the shelves.[13] His bright products, he hoped, would act on the passing housewife quickly, like a "mousetrap," grabbing her attention as she moved between aisles.[14] An understanding of the sheer speed of supermarket shopping, confirmed by the primary research of his California lab, thus informed Landor's work. He understood that the wheels of the cart implied a certain haste, accelerating customers into a new temporal norm and upping the pace by which their "feminine" impulses might be acted upon.

As such Landor saw that in the new space of the supermarket, impulse buys were accelerating, one such purchase always leading straight to the next. His awareness of this acceleration led him into acts of design which harnessed and amplified it. It was as though he had realized that the exclamatory signs which others found insulting and infantilizing ("Serve Yourself!" or "Look!") were overexcited not just because their creators held a low opinion of female intelligence but, paradoxically, because they knew that the women (and men) shopping in their stores were being bombarded with multiple messages and that they would need to shout at them if their message was to have any hope of getting through. Landor sought to provoke similar stimulations—stimulations which continued to appeal to the visual but which, like those exclamation marks, did so to spur an impulsive action: to draw the eye in order to draw the hand in turn.

This determination had a decisive influence on the characteristic size and shape of supermarket packaging. One of the most important approaches involved Landor's inventive use of cellophane. Although he was far from alone in his innovations, Landor had a huge impact on reintroducing transparent panels to a shopping environment which had long been reducing its use of glass windows and displays. As fridges lost their doors and were thrown open to passing customers, and as many supermarkets swapped their old glass frontages for brick and concrete exteriors, it was as though Landor took the unwanted glass panels, smashed them into a thousand pieces, and then applied them carefully to the surface of all the individual packages his firm designed. Maybe that glass had now turned into a plastic wrap, and maybe it now invited customers not into an alluring habitable space but into the internal and miniature world of food itself. But rumors of what Bowlby has called the "death of the window" were, from Landor's point of view, exaggerated.[15] As a 1955 article in *Good Packaging* commented:

Imaginative design treatment has evolved a dramatic new concept in the use of cellophane.... [One] major project was ... Granny Goose Dip Chips, a rippled chip. Here the accent was on design treatment to convey the product's primary purpose to customers at sight. The imaginative solution to this problem involves what is believed to be a new approach to transparent packaging. An oval corner window, the only unprinted area on the polymer-coated cellophane, is set in the center of a realistically photographed Lazy Susan laden with appetizing dip. It gives the chips the tantalizing look of being contained in a bowl. To reinforce this "mirage" a single chip, showing scooping into one of the dips, draws the consumer into the picture.[16]

Or as Landor himself put it, "properly designed cellophane packaging reaches people deep down in their subconscious where the heart strings release the purse strings." The value of these transparent ovals, triangles, and squares, for him, thus lay in their capacity to trigger rapid impulses in supermarket shoppers, allowing his clients "to move" their "products faster off the shelf." At times Landor would even revive the old metaphor of driving invoked in early descriptions of the first supermarkets, noting that "billboards are not finished.... There are still fluorescent inks on soap cartons and other items." Yet his constant awareness of the propulsion of the cart's wheels also led him to recognize the limits to the analogy: if he was sometimes designing indoor billboards, then they also needed to be portable—roadside signs his cart drivers could still reach out and grab.

His awareness of the "volumetric" cart's constant presence thus led him to rethink the shape and weight of the packages he created. Landor saw that it was not enough to replace a subtle palette and tasteful aesthetics with garish colors or other arresting visual designs. His brief, extending beyond the visual, also required him to consider the shape and weight of the packaging objects he designed. He needed to ensure that once a customer acted to grab a passing item, it needed to be easy to lift. In consequence, as though in a belated counterpoint to the wheels that had grown from the bellies of the supermarket baskets, individual items now sprouted handles. Some of these handles were overt; over the 1950s, commissions of Landor Associates and other packaging firms introduced cardboard handles for multipacks of beer and donuts, for example. Others were more subtle: Landor gave Nalley's Lumberjack Syrup an "hourglass shape"; ensured that the twisted handles of loaves of bread would be available to the passing customer; and did what he could to make his redesign of a V8 bottle lighter than its original "hefty 68g."[17]

This elaborate reorientation of supermarket goods and supermarket space thus sought to lure the customer into a series of accelerated buying gestures predicated on an always-moving and always-inviting cart. Landor used some traditional imperatives of spectacle and even revived the commercial use of enticing windows, but only after he pressed both into a tense and volatile alliance with the supermarket's countervailing commitment to keep its goods and its people on the move. The result of this project was the production of that Latourian space of today: that supermarket in which one's acts of subscription, or voluntary engagement, can quickly lead to an experience of manipulation and a loss of control. Landor, like other designers behind the scenes in the supermarket, did much to make it a place of wonder, full of beautiful uniformity, enticing tiny windows, and the image of a bounty beyond the dreams of earlier historical epochs. Yet he also recognized and intensified the fact that the minute they stepped into it, his customers were ushered along and toward the exit at new haste, and all the better for them to succumb to impulses beyond domestic budget planning.

Understanding the work of Landor and Goldman among other influential supermarket designers thus frequently requires us to call attention to objects and developments which are usually overlooked or regarded as unimportant or spontaneous. Throughout its history key elements within the supermarket system have been considered natural or unplanned or to occupy a realm beyond ideology. For example, when he suggested that postwar US supermarkets were "unpatentable," Milton Friedman identified them as a key physical counterpart of his academic system of "positive economics," a naturalizing system which likewise purported to deal only with "what is" and to be, as Thomas I. Palley suggests, "value-free and unaffected by ... the values of the society in which the theorist works."[18] His emphasis on the sheer unpatentable obviousness of the supermarket as such reflected a more general tendency to see the culture of consumer capitalism as a spontaneous force and to insist that the role of government was not to regulate but to get out of the way of its free and natural flow. And in this respect, although Friedman sometimes distanced himself from the polemical provocations of Frederic Hayek or Ayn Rand, the emphasis he placed on the sheer obviousness and inevitability of the supermarket reflected his underlying agreement with Rand's feeling that capitalism as a whole was ultimately rooted not in culture but nature, and possessed a unique capacity to harness "the basic, metaphysical fact of man's nature—the connection between his survival and his use of reason."[19]

This, in practice, encouraged an assumption that the global success of the supermarket system was spontaneous, part of a natural outflow of individual freedoms first spawned in the democratic heartlands of the United States. The old Soviet tendency to exempt carts and other items from the capitalist culture that spawned them and to see them as natural or universal instead found a powerful echo in the more general neoliberal tendency to see the supermarket sector as a natural outflow of a universal commercial impulse. The international reach of such stores, for US capitalism's champions, often seemed only to consummate latent freedoms, manifesting what Ronald Reagan called a spirit of "free enterprise" and "economic vitality" which was "broad-based and irreversible" and which emanated not "from the top, but from the bottom."[20] As we gain a settled historical perspective on US consumer capitalism's triumphant postwar era, however, it becomes increasingly easy to see the ideological work being performed by a phrase like "economic vitality" among other classic Reaganite figurations. For such familiar neoliberal phrases, in naturalizing "free" trade, also spirited attention away from the sheer hard work that lay behind global consumerism, disguising both its reliance on government regulation and the extent to which it was designed into existence by gifted artists like Landor. Moreover, as neoliberalism's rhetorical habits of self-naturalization and self-neutralization become increasingly apparent to us, so it also becomes clear that future critiques need to consider not only the famously global brands but the inconspicuous structures in which such brands have historically sat and operated. Of equal interest now are those capitalist modes of design which preferred to sit in the background, blending into a naturalized environment which seemed to function on the level of impulse or instinct.

The naturalness of the cart and its central position in Landor's transformation of the supermarket foodscape reverberate in an important moment from Cormac McCarthy's 2006 novel *The Road*. In one famous scene, as McCarthy's father and son push a cart full of their possessions south, they chance upon a ruined store:

> On the outskirts of the city they came to a supermarket.... They left their cart in the lot and walked the littered aisles. In the produce section in the bottom of the bins they found a few ancient runner beans and what looked to have once been apricots, long dried to wrinkled effigies of themselves. The boy followed behind. They pushed out through the rear door. In the alleyway behind the store a few shopping carts, all badly rusted. They went back through the store again looking for another cart but there were none. By the door there were two softdrink machines that had been tilted over into the floor and opened with a prybar. Coins everywhere in the ash. He sat and ran his hand around in the works of the gutted machines and in the second one it closed over a cold metal cylinder. He withdrew his hand slowly and sat looking at a Coca Cola.
> What is it, Papa?
> It's a treat. For you.
> What is it?
> Here. Sit down.... He leaned his nose to the slight fizz coming from the can and then handed it to the boy. Go ahead, he said.
> The boy took the can. It's bubbly, he said.
> Go ahead.
> He looked at his father and then tilted the can and drank. He sat there thinking about it. It's really good, he said.
> Yes. It is. (19–20)

At a key juncture of his essay sequence *One-Way Street* (1928), Walter Benjamin relates the history of print culture to the distinctive atmosphere he knew firsthand from Kurfürstendamm among the other major Berlin thoroughfares of the Weimar era. Script, he said, had long ago "found in the book a refuge." Words had found a home on paper, and the eyes of readers had grown adept at following them down a series of horizontal lines. But in the full sweep of history, Benjamin suggests, the "refuge" of the book was limited, a rarity at most. Lithography and newspaper layout always led words and eyes alike in opposite directions. Our darting eyes, zigzagging and circling to absorb the scattered content of a front page or billboard, have always struggled to keep up with the dispersions of a printed language that the book alone allowed us to control. Outside, on railway station walls, in the arcades of the belle époque, or along Kurfürstendamm itself, print is more familiarly "dragged ... onto the street," scattered through "advertisements," and "subjected to the brutal heteronomies of economic chaos." As this dispersal intensifies, eyes everywhere must "read more in the vertical than in the horizontal plane," even obeying "the dictatorial perpendicular" to decipher the codes and graffiti and propaganda in which the walls of Benjamin's city hinted at what it would soon become. And so, "before a child of our time finds his way clear to opening a book, his eyes have been exposed to such a blizzard of changing, colourful, conflicting letters that the chances of his penetrating the archaic stillness of the book are slight."[21] Dual prophecies are given. Benjamin understands that the "hour ... dedicated to the executioner" is drawing near, but his essay already looks beyond the coming terror and toward a modern or postwar culture in which "horizontal" reading has been more completely superseded by a kind of superficial scanning of information.

"One-Way Street," then, looks ahead to the intensification of the textual "blizzard" that has been a feature of the postmodern and internet eras. It anticipates the complex arrangements of panels and tiles by which not only websites and user screens but TV news channels, shop windows, billboards, and even restaurant menus now echo the influence of the newspapers of the recent past. But while elsewhere Benjamin famously quotes Paul

Valery's prophecy of a time when "we shall be supplied with pictures or sound sequences... at the touch of a button," any suggestion that the "dictatorial perpendicular" might one day become tactile remains only dim.[22] And yet this is the very transformation that a range of American photographers have made apparent in their treatment of the supermarket. During a break from his familiar world of 1950s Washington politics, for example, the photographer Thomas J. O'Halloran captures a supermarket full of text. The female shoppers in his photographs are above all readers, explicators who must decipher their weekly budgeted needs from the vertical and horizontal axes of the supermarket's jagged walls. Yet what O'Halloran's photos also make apparent, of course, is that the shopper must reach into this figurative newspaper, pulling the signified out of each signifier that she reaches out to grab. Benjamin's blizzard continues unabated in O'Halloran's photographed foodscape. But it also now acquires a tactile element, accelerating Valery's gestures in a restless scanning and stretching which thus began in the supermarket but which today we repeat in all sorts of other commercial contexts, and especially online. And the more or less unspoken object which allows this rapid repetition of impulse buys is the cart that the shopper pushes in front of her: a cart which, whether pixelated or built of steel, offers us the void into which we can pour the multivalent fragments of materialized text that we want or need to bring into our lives.

On the floor of *The Road*'s abandoned supermarket, however, the blizzard stops. A kind of historical reversal takes place. We travel back even to a period before that captured in John Vachon's image of a grocery store in Nebraska in which handwritten signs compete with commodified boxes, posters, and cans. Food in McCarthy's ruined store instead loses abstract

Figure 11. "Shopping in Supermarket," 1957, Thomas O'Halloran Jr.

Figure 12. "Shopping in Supermarket," 1957, Thomas O'Halloran Jr.

Figure 13. Grand Grocery, Lincoln, Nebraska, 1942, John Vachon.

signification of any kind. The boy focuses on a single, miraculous drink without knowing what it is. Coca-Cola—a resonant brand which for Slavoj Žižek epitomizes our culture of hedonism, always promising and never giving satisfaction—loses the textuality that carries this tantalizing effect.[23] Some fleeting joy unexpectedly returns to the ruined supermarket. The end of the blizzard returns the father and the son to themselves and their life together, allowing the son to experience a satisfaction which, Žižek suggests, we would understand as a "melancholic experience" that marks "a loss of desire itself." It is easy to read *The Road*'s sudden blast of Edenic energy solely through the prism of the resonant commodity which thus loses its branding and regains objective value in the counter. Coca-Cola certainly signifies much here. But it is also noticeable that the scene only arrives at this moment of possibility after a series of marked and underscored abandonment to carts. Carts are rejected here, left outside, or deemed useless due to rust. It is no surprise to encounter such omissions: carts, as we have seen, often pass unnoticed. But the still and horizontal lines of McCarthy's prose also stagger and reiterate this rejection of the cart in such a way as to associate its disappearance with Coke's reacquisition of bodily satisfaction. Coke can become again "a pause that refreshes," it seems, just so long as it escapes the cart's yawning void.

Exit

In 1973, when the Welsh scholar Raymond Williams traveled to California for a visiting professorship at Stanford University, the supermarket industry which had first emerged in that state half a century beforehand was reaching new heights of success. The streamlined store layout and packaging designs first developed by Landor Associates and Kroger among other leading companies in the 1950s had by now become standard features of most larger supermarkets, and the gradual rollout of new barcode technology seemed to promise even smoother shopping experiences to come. Reflecting this dominance, US films and novels of the period often adopted supermarkets as a setting, sometimes treating their aisles as if they were the new park bench—as places of crowded anonymity where spies and strangers might meet—and sometimes as epicenters of a plenitude now grown banal, processed, drained of promise.[1] In other 1970s stories supermarkets seem agents of homogenization, becoming identical coordinates which erode geographical or other differences even as they help a given character navigate them. Halfway through a road trip out West, the protagonist of Don DeLillo's countercultural *Americana* (1971) falls with some relief upon a lone supermarket, thrilling at its gondolas full of "thunderbolts" and "rectangles of evangelistic writ," and even finding reassurance in the familiar "nudging, ... testing and prodding" of the shopping carts behind him as he walks through its "spangled ark."[2] In Stanley Elkin's *The Franchiser* (1976), too, the supermarket becomes the main material in the "packed masonry of America," a standard architectural feature now so common across the land that his hero can no longer tell Birmingham, Alabama, and Birmingham, Indiana, apart, knowing only that on the "rich topsoil of city asphalt" in both "he feels he is home."[3] Other writers still, decades before McCarthy published *The Road*, already thrilled at the thought of a future when "dandelion and milkweed will struggle through" such "blacktop."[4] As such, Ira Levin's *The Stepford Wives* (1972) can seem only a particularly speculative variation on a theme that became widespread in US literature during the decade. Many painted a similar picture of an America grown full of supermarkets, and of supermarkets grown full of housewives, all of them strolling along filling their carts before driving back to the menacing perfection of their vast suburban homes.

Another clear message from US culture in this period is that when you go along to a supermarket, you never quite know who you will meet. At one unnamed store in the 1960s the soul singer Eugene McDaniels encounters a fellow shopper who harangues him after she notices, "You ain't even white."[5] At others since the summer of 1977, either elsewhere in the US or far beyond its borders, Elvis has been seen alive, browsing the aisles for jam and bacon and peanut butter to make his all-time favorite sandwich. Legends of this kind, in confirming that the supermarket had become a ubiquitous and even unavoidable feature of modern life, make it seem likely that Williams would have ended up in one at some point during his California sabbatical. Perhaps, if he had done so, he would have paid little attention to the molded plastic jars and cans ranged before him. In a year that would see him publish not only *The Country and the City* but also his *New Left Review* essay "Base and Superstructure in Marxist Cultural Theory," he clearly had too much on his mind to be distracted by what Elkin called "the quotidian acts of the market basket and shopping cart."[6] All the same, during his stay at Stanford Williams did absorb other aspects of ordinary California, and his subsequent reflections on this most formative of postmodern landscapes can deepen our understanding of the shopping cart that had grown so central to it. The encounter with the Los Angeles freeway that he would recollect in his vatic *Towards 2000* (1983) holds especially rich resonances for life behind the cart. As he observed:

> Looked at from right outside, the traffic flows and their regulation are clearly a social order of a determined kind, yet what is experienced inside them—in the conditioned atmosphere and internal music of this windowed shell—is movement, choice of direction, the pursuit of self-determined private purposes. All the other shells are moving, in comparable ways but for their own different private ends. They are not so much other people, in any full sense, but other units that signal and are signaled to, so that private mobilities can proceed safely and relatively unhindered. And if all this is seen from the outside as in deep ways determined, or in some sweeping glance as dehumanised, that is not at all how it feels inside the shell, with people you want to be with going where you want to go.[7]

With such observations, as Paul Gilroy has recognized, Williams became "among the first commentators to grasp the significance" of what he called "mobile privatisation." Realizing that "the increased privatisation of life ... was being combined with an unprecedented degree of mobility," Wiliams's *Towards 2000* "used the image of modern car traffic to capture the deadly ambiguities in this combination, which, he felt, characterised the whole unsettling experience of being in a consumer society."[8] The open and unlocated nature of his description certainly recognizes that the tensions of modern city traffic are not peculiar to California but are becoming symptomatic of a global landscape based on groupable forms of individual passion. Indeed, Williams's vivid everyday description strongly suggests that if he had followed one of these "windowed shells" right up until it parked in a single painted space, *Towards 2000* could also have illuminated for us the transformations and tensions that occur when we swap a steering wheel for the handle of a shopping cart. The empathy built into his critique of traffic flow certainly stands in contrast to those passing references to the supermarket which I have considered earlier in this essay and which treat it chiefly as a mere metonym or symbol of late globalization. Indeed, in omitting detail and indulging in negative polemic, Giorgio Agamben and Jean Baudrillard's denunciations of the supermarket as a "Land of Cockayne" might seem to echo the hyperbole of the supermarket industry itself, accepting its self-fulfilling assumptions of global invincibility alongside its claims of variety and choice, and disagreeing only insofar as this causes them dread. A third theoretician, the Paris anthropologist Marc Augé, at least lingers long enough to see the supermarket through the eyes of those ordinary "habitué[s]" otherwise known as you and me. Here Augé finds a quintessential postmodern "nonplace" and an end of human connection—a world where "slot machines and credit cards communicate wordlessly, through gestures, with an abstract, unmediated commerce: a world thus surrendered to solitary individuality."[9] Yet even Augé only echoes *Towards 2000*'s concern with *privatisation*; he does not continue the kind of patient observation which then leads Williams to his crucial modifier *mobile*. Augé, like Baudrillard and Agamben, effectively defers to the industry's own description of itself, agreeing that the supermarket is a kind of brilliant delivery machine, stunning and complex, and disagreeing only insofar as he blames such efficiencies for our deepening isolation.

On the other hand, Williams, in his account of modern traffic, remains at once more attentive and more skeptical. He seems interested less in the implications of a known and familiar myth than in the lived reality behind it. What he makes evident, thanks to this more practical approach, is the role our choices and indeed our agency play in the determined social form. Not unlike Bruno Latour—and in keeping with the guarded balance between individual action and social hegemony which he would strike in the pages of *New Left Review* while still in California— Williams's focus falls on those emotions and desires that are at once the very stuff of individuality and the cause of its absorption into the behavior of the group. All manner of individual impulses here draw us into the herd. But even when we submit to it, joining a steady stream of traffic, few of us feel that we are thus submitting to a cliché. Clearly we merge into what Siegfried Kracaeur once called a "mass ornament," an urban carriageway "composed of thousands of bodies."[10] Yet the "windowed shell" in which we sit ensures that the crowd remains at arm's length. Our ornamentalization and our egocentrism go hand in hand. As certain drivers around us mutter, gesticulate, swear, tailgate, jump in lines, and beep their horns, they clearly do regard their fellow motorists as little more than "other units that signal and are signaled to." But what happens when these paradoxical machines, at once antlike and egotistic, find their way into a supermarket parking lot? What happens when we leave our shells behind—when drivers swap their semiprivate cars for the X-ray-like revelations of the open supermarket cart?

The feelings that run through our minds when we walk toward a supermarket entrance are far more intense than some admit. As we approach our Latourian "preformatting" in our chain store of choice, we become a mess of unfinished thoughts. We scuttle through the parking lot, old coupons blowing out of our recycled bags, and we brace ourselves for the complicated job ahead. We might feel inside our pockets for our shopping list. But no doubt we are under no illusions of finding everything on it, or of avoiding all impulse buys. Too many distractions are already in play. The ATM outside might have brought bad news, forcing upon us new and challenging calculations. Our small children might be crying, freezing before the dreaded child seat. Our older children might be treating us like Siri, asking us endless questions, lobbying for sugar. Like the sound of a distant abattoir, some appalling pop track might be beeping and squawking at us from the invisible speakers inside. And all the while we know that in there, the supermarket's textual "blizzard" is lying in wait, ready to smother us with its daily bewilderments, its unanticipated multibuys and counterintuitive prices, its defrosted stale bread and unusable Best Before dates, all complicating further the difficult work of buying food on a budget.

As a result, when we wrench a supermarket cart from its horizontal row, we might even feel a little relief. The cart is not a life raft, and no one clings to it for dear life. But there are small pleasures to be had in laying claim to one, in setting its wheels in motion and guiding it into empty space, and there are reassurances, too, in the barrier it places between us and the new commercial kingdom, this erstwhile "palace of plenty," into which we push it. Our cart, admittedly, falls short of the hermetic cell on offer in a private car. A shell has an occupant, according to Gaston Bachelard, a dweller to whom it affords "maximum repose."[11] Most car ads today alight upon a single car, pull it out of the traffic, revel in its new Hi-Fi and Wi-Fi capabilities, and then urge upon us its safety in terms that have nothing to do with good visibility or care for pedestrians and everything to do with how it would protect its passengers in the event of an accident. Unlike this ultimate human shell, sold in denial of its own mass reproduction, a borrowed cart will always seem something of a leveler, exposing private lifestyles to the world. Yet it can still feel protective, a shield if not a shell. It is simple; it asks no submission from us; it demands no new skills. It welcomes us into the easiest of all possible Latourian "alliances." A moving barrier brought under our control, it carries all our consumer choices, allowing us to lose ourselves in our own lives. It lets us pursue our domestic passions while helping us avoid and even forget those we follow or who follow us.

In consequence, under the glare of the supermarket's LED lights, we ourselves enact mobile privatization in effect. Cars and carts alike give us protection "from the outside world" while granting "unprecedented access to it," in Stephen Groening's phrase.[12] These two machines, however—one fueled and one unfueled—achieve this common object in radically different ways. Mobile privatization is now acquiring optimal form on our roads. If drivers have long been "excused from normal etiquette and face-to-face interactions," as John Urry suggested, then cruise control, automatic parking, and other new servomechanisms now allow many to pay even less notice to other motorists and pedestrians.[13] Up and down the aisles of our local supermarket it is a different story. Here we might still resemble "juxtaposed atoms," in

Henri Lefebvre's phrase, our isolation still flowing out of our own emotional deliberations, and remaining difficult to overlook.[14] "The triumph of mounting mileage," as Theodor Adorno suggested, deflects the idea of "running ... from one's own body" while "at the same time effortlessly surpassing it"; the fastest on the road are not always the fastest on foot, nor the most alert those with the best eyesight.[15] Once we step inside a supermarket, on the other hand, a sort of incomplete bodily restoration occurs. We stand and walk through its aisles; we use our own strength to push our own stuff along; and we reach out for more of it with our own hands. Yet even as we lift and place and rearrange and wrap and transfer the products that will sustain our own lives, the supermarket keeps ushering us toward commodities that we know are available to all. The general pattern in which our own individual actions fit—unlike that of urban traffic—cannot be ignored. Evidence of our mobile privatization remains palpable, felt; we hold it in our own hands. Even as we do so, however, even as we peer into our cart and review the proof of our own predictability, there are still comforts to be had. All our cans and cartons and bottles and packages might now feel handled, piled on top of each other, and no longer quite so new as when they first beckoned to us from the shelves. Our original plans might be long gone, our costs spiraling out of control. Our bread might be squashed and the apples might be bruised. But they are, at least, ours—or will be soon. They are proof our life still trundles on. Plenitude, for the time being, remains in reach.

Other 1970s fictions, unlike *The Franchiser* and *Americana,* approach the contemporary rise of the supermarket from oblique and unexpected angles. At the start of the decade, before he became embroiled in a succession of ugly literary disputes, John Gardner drew upon his interest in medieval writing to produce his revisionist narrative *Grendel* (1971). Written in the first person, this novel gives both a voice and a rationale to the half human cannibal at the heart of the Middle English poem *Beowulf*. Lines of identification are complicated as a result. Whereas the original *Beowulf* casts Grendel as a clawed demon, a monster who despoils a Christian world "blessed with abundance," such Manichean certainties vanish as Gardner has his hungering narrator catalogue the sadism and violence of the Danemen themselves as well as those moments when they preyed on him.[16] This almost Miltonic disruption of understood moral relations then leads *Grendel* to regard the plenitude of the Danemen's world not as a sign of their providence or grace but in a mood of righteous bewilderment. Strongholds of civil goodness in *Beowulf* itself, their mead halls become grotesque, idolatrous hubs of orgiastic excess. From earlier raids for human food Grendel remembers that the "inside walls" of the Danemen's mead halls were "beautifully painted and hung with tapestries, and every cross-timber and falcon's perch was carved and geegawed with toads, snakes, dragon shapes, deer, cows, pigs, trees, trolls."[17] Although *Grendel* then accepts from *Beowulf* that the most opulent mead hall of all belongs to the "liegelord" Hrothgar, Gardner also makes a significant adjustment. His Hrothgar owes his power not just to the arbitrary blessings of royal birth emphasized in *Beowulf*, but also to his ambition and kindling of new strategies. In *Grendel*'s retelling, indeed, he might even seem a self-made man. Soon he begins

> to outstrip the rest. He'd worked out a theory about what the fighting was for, and now he no longer fought with his six closest neighbors. He'd shown them the strength of his organization, and now, instead of making war on them, he sent men to them every three

months or so, with heavy wagons and back-slings, to gather their tribute to his greatness. They piled his wagon high with gold and leather and weapons, and they kneeled to his messengers and made long speeches and promised to defend him against any foolhardy outlaw that dared to attack him. Hrothgar's messengers answered with friendly words and praise of the men they'd just plundered, as if the whole thing had been his idea, then whipped up the oxen, pulled up their loaded back-slings, and started home. It was a hard trip. The tall, silky grass of the meadows and the paths along the forest would clog the heavy wagon spokes and snarl the oxen's hooves.... Sometimes a horse, mired to the waist, would give up and merely stand, head hanging, as if waiting for death, and the men would howl at it and cut it with whips, or throw stones, or club it with heavy limbs, until finally one of them came to his senses and calmed the others, and they would winch out the horse with ropes and wagon wheels, if they could, or else abandon the horse or kill it—first stripping off the saddle and bridle and the handsomely decorated harness....

Hrothgar met with his council for many nights and days, and they drank and talked and prayed to their curious carved-out creatures and finally came to a decision. They built roads. The kings from whom they'd taken tributes of treasure they now asked for tributes of men. Then Hrothgar and his neighbors, loaded like ants on a long march, pushed foot by foot and day by day around the marshes and over the moors and through the woods, pressing flat rocks into soft ground and grass, and packing smaller stones around the rocks' sides, until, from my watch on the wall of the cliff, Hrothgar's whole realm was like a wobbly, lopsided wheel with spokes of stone.[18]

Written in an age of monopolies, when national chains were absorbing smaller rivals at an ever-faster rate, *Grendel*'s new thoughts on feudal conquest invite contemporary parallels. Sometimes the novel verges on outright allegory. *They built roads*, its shortest sentence, also departs from *Beowulf* itself, and bluntly modernizes that poem's original insistence on sail and ship as the source of Hrothgar's power. Yet this overt American echo is isolated and a little unusual. Gardner more generally avoids such direct mirrors of past and present. Elsewhere, when these parallels impress themselves upon his narrative, one can feel him casting around for new confusions. Sudden bursts of medieval argot, synesthetic disorientation, and formal experiment all hold allegory at bay. Overall Gardner resists the temptations of historical parallelism. He often sabotages the echoes he encounters between his now and *Beowulf*'s then. When he compares "Hrothgar's whole realm" to "a wobbly, lopsided wheel with spokes of stone," his description might recall the coordinated road networks of contemporary supermarkets—as we have seen in Walmart's first distribution point, Jameson's "hidden utopia," opened in Bentonville, Alabama, in 1970—but it might also recall capitalistic appropriation in general.[19] All the while it remains encased in a medieval terrain full of mud and dying horses and altogether less solid than our own.

In this way *Grendel* brings about a careful but unmistakable temporalization of its source. Hrothgar here seems a harbinger of the coming capitalism. His demands, his impressments, and his expansionist aims all suggest that his new roads are no isolated occurrence but inaugurate an industrializing tendency which will eventually propel us into a modern era where (for Antonio Negri and Michael Hardt) "all of nature has become capital" and all of the United States (for *The Franchiser*) has become asphalt.[20] A similar temporal alchemy leaves Grendel vestigial, prehistoric. No longer embodying a Manichean evil one must accept as an everlasting presence in our world, he becomes a creature Hrothgar's advancements would leave behind, and more reminiscent of those monsters whom, in

Steven Shaviro's words, we might "think of... as archaic beings, oozing out of our primordial imaginings."[21] His unruliness expels him from Hrothgar's violent progressive world.

His own violence often upholds this dichotomy. *Grendel* glories in gore and suffering. "I held up the guard to taunt them, then held him still higher and leered into his face.... As if casually, in plain sight of them all, I bit his head off, crunched through the helmet and skull with my teeth and, holding the jerking, blood-slippery body in two hands, sucked the blood that sprayed like a hot, thick geyser from his neck. It got all over me."[22] His raw cannibalism, however, always exists in parallel with other consuming passions. As he spies on his human quarry in the mead halls, and as they drink mead until they can no longer stand, Gardner's Grendel sees them attack each other without good reason and slaughter animals without regard to food. The teleology of progress that *Grendel* imposes upon *Beowulf* thus gets disrupted as Gardner upsets received ideas of what is civilized and what is savage. When he kills, Grendel kills without mercy—but he always kills to eat. When he eats, he eats indelicately—but he always eats because he is hungry. Alone among *Grendel*'s cast he is afraid that he might "starve to death."[23] Among his human victims, on the other hand, the drinking of mead—a drink they drink to get drunk long after it has quenched their thirst—becomes paradigmatic of all their impulsive acting on desire. All they consume they consume as drunks drink mead, approaching the world before them in a spirit not of need but of desires which they mistake for need. They overlook dead potential food and they kill creatures they would never eat.

> It was late spring. Food was plentiful. Every sheep and goat had its wobbly twins, the forest was teeming, and the first crops of the hillsides were coming into fruit. A man would roar, "I'll steal their gold

and burn their mead-hall!" shaking his sword as if the tip were afire....

Then once, around midnight, I came to a hall in ruins. The cows in their pens lay burbling blood through their nostrils, with javelin holes in their necks. None had been eaten. The watchdogs lay like dark wet stones, with their heads cut off, teeth bared. The fallen hall was a square of flames and acrid smoke, and the people inside (none of them had been eaten either) were burned black, small, like dwarfs turned dark and crisp.... There was no sign of the gold they'd kept—not so much as a melted hilt.[24]

Some years earlier, toward the end of *The Long Revolution* (1961), Raymond Williams detected a subtle shift in British English speech. In discussions of macroeconomics and the market, he noted, the traditional usage *customers* was ceding ground to *consumers; consumption* and *consumerism* were becoming default terms. As befitted a scholar whose fascination with ordinary language would eventually culminate in *Keywords* (1976), Williams felt that *consumer* and *consumption*'s new "popularity" deserved "more attention." *Consumer*, he thought, "unconsciously expresses a really very odd and partial version of the purpose of economic activity," and not least because "the image is drawn from the furnace or the stomach, yet how many things there are we neither eat nor burn." Having identified in *consumer* a metaphoric capacity to regard all we use as food—and hence to equate use itself with gastrointestinal destruction—Williams then illustrates his point by turning not just to those inedible commodities which would seem able to fulfill this metaphoric tendency but, intriguingly, to individual foods too. *Drinka Pinta Milka day:* a piece of dubious dietary advice, this 1950s advertising slogan's appearance in *The Long Revolution* also reveals that, for Williams, the new logic of consumption has not only found in food a useful structuring metaphor but has also looped back and found in it another commercial field to conquer. Even for industries based on the demand and supply of actual calories, in other words, the semantic shift toward *consumption* continues to orchestrate a movement away from "known demands" one might have traced to the stomach and toward a market designed to ensure "that we consume what industry finds it convenient to produce." He continues:

> If we were not consumers, but users, we might look at society very differently, for the concept of use involves general human judgements, ... whereas consumption, with its crude hand-to-mouth patterns, tends to cancel these questions, replacing them by the stimulated and controlled absorption of the products of an external and autonomous system.[25]

The Williams of *The Long Revolution* could still suggest that "we have not gone all the way with this new tendency, and are still in a position to reverse it."[26] But his confidence in our capacity to bring about such a reversal would not last long. By the time he published *Keywords* in 1976, his tone had grown more jaded, and more resigned to the fact that *consumption* and *consumer* had now become our "predominant descriptive nouns for all kinds of use of goods and services."[27] All of *consumer* and *consumption*'s "unfavourable" connotations as such remained visible to him, and in the definitions of *Keywords* he could continue to show how their habitual usage in market analysis and everyday conversation was blurring ideas of use and destruction together, leading us to a cultural or unconscious feeling in which it no longer seemed possible to touch objects without also causing them harm. Yet his tone of resignation also now carries a suspicion—a fear that he can only detect this blurring of use and destruction because he can recollect an earlier cultural phase, before globalization, when consumers remained customers and could act on satiable desire rather than some recurring impulse to vaporize or burn. Viewing the new formation in the dying light of the old, his simple word choices reveal a premonition that the semantic shift he is describing might soon become so ubiquitous as to seem natural and unavailable to critique. His fear is of bearing witness to a linguistic distortion of object use at precisely the moment in which it becomes too normal to see.

Use becomes destructive in *Grendel* too. The violence of Hrothgar and his men clearly results from far more than an immediate or strategic need to defeat their enemies or flaunt their imperial strength. Instead it seems to shadow their basic and fundamental engagements with the world. It seems to reflect a reordering of desire, answering impulses which mead has awoken in them but cannot sate. Soon after their first mouthfuls of the stuff, *Grendel* finds them looking around, drunk, almost passionlessly launching themselves against women and each other. Their forays abroad, as they flow down the "spokes" of Hrothgar's "lopsided wheel," surging into other halls all around, seem to reflect a similar feeling of being thwarted or being set upon an eternal search. When Grendel bites the head off his victim and sucks "the blood that sprayed like a hot, thick geyser from his neck," his makeshift drink offers him total satisfaction; he eats nothing else for days. As they carry out beheadings of their own, however, Hrothgar's men do so without thought and as if in a recurring reflex. Against Grendel's cannibal need they succumb to desire, racing from one torpid death to another, never looking back. They abandon their enemies and "watchdogs" to rot on the ground, as they move toward the next mead hall. They never pause to drink from the "javelin holes" that they leave in the necks of the dead cows. Numb automatic violence: the virus inside Hrothgar and his men is akin to the infections of that Žižekian regime in which pleasure becomes a "weird duty" or "obligation" and the promise of satisfaction can only threaten "the melancholy termination of desire."[28] Sweeping on, giving no thought to what they leave behind them, they just focus on finding some new outlet for their impulses—but only in order that they might abandon it in turn.

The contrast again calls *The Road* (2006) to mind. Waste there too surpasses cannibalism among other forms of savagery. A sin worse than sadism flourishes in the heart of the civilized world. For the apocalypse pulsing from some unknown epicenter in *The Road* might remain unexplained, but its consequences always eclipse the bestiality it unleashes. It burns cities, destroys mothers, annihilates childhood; it dwarfs the lone cannibals whom it sets loose upon the world. Yet that ruination also allows *The Road*'s father and son to take a slower route around the supermarket and even to secure a sudden capacity to pause and sit down on its empty linoleum floor. Earlier in the novel they were hunted; as they pushed their cart down a road they hoped would lead to the unlikely refuge of "the south," they scoped the world around them for signs of danger, scanning left and right not unlike shoppers rushing through a supermarket of today. Now, as they come upon the ruins of one such store, they gain respite, and the novel stretches plausibility as they leave their cart outside and slow down and inspect its "littered aisles" at their own pace.[29] In consequence, they find treasure: an edible relic leftover from the lost plenty—and the son, decelerated and liberated from the knowledge of what Coke is, can really "enjoy a pause that refreshes." He can use rather than consume the drink, and it can replenish him just as "a small colony of ... morels" will later and just as human blood replenishes Grendel.[30] Unhurried, for a precious moment he and his father no longer seem so compelled to rush as if from one consumerist impulse to another. Yet all the while Hrothgar's men trundle on. Not even peeping into the carcasses they leave behind, they seem always driven toward their next thwarting, their violence unmoored from all horizons of need. They lack the moral prerequisites of sadism or perversion—cannot divulge what their "fighting was for." They can only peel the world away, forever peering into the metafictive void for a missing element they dare not hope find. They languish under "some kind of curse," subjects of everlasting desire.

Ruin, in both *Grendel* and *The Road,* is thus modern, the fault of those beholden to what Frédéric Lordon has called capitalism's *"regime of desire,"* or *"epithumé"* (from the Greek *epithumia,* or desire), in which a ceaseless demand for more lays waste to the world, destroying mud and concrete alike.[31] The strongest echoes of both works are thus to be found not in the war or lawless zones of our age but in the circuits of mass consumerism that reach into the kitchens and computer screens of our own homes. When slavery, ecological waste, and human suffering all arise not from ideological hatred or geopolitical competition but from the implacable demands of human desire, as is the case in *Grendel* and *The Road,* the immediate parallel lies with the commodities that almost all of us continue to pile into our carts online or in-store. For all the waste products bound up in those commodities—their sculpted polyethylene wrappings, their cellophane windows and cardboard flaps and tabs, their superabundance of sugar, meat, and fat—of course bear huge responsibility for the slow apocalypse otherwise known as the Anthropocene.[32] And in the cart's "volumetric" void, as we have seen, there is always room for more: more of the nitrogen extraction and human trafficking required to reap the fruit and vegetable crops of Europe and North America; more of the destruction of rainforests and freshwater ecosystems now required to feed the yearlong thirst of sugarcane and produce enough of it to meet demand; more of the billions of plastic bags and plastic bottles which fall into rivers and seas every year.[33] It is no wonder that when, in a later visit to a second abandoned store, *The Road*'s father opens "the door of a walk-in cooler," he should suddenly recoil from it as "the sour rank smell of the dead washed out of the darkness."[34] Putrefaction's sudden eruption into a shopping space once designed to eliminate all but the most appealing odors is an apt metaphor for the tides of human and nonhuman waste hidden amid the utopian promise of supermarket flow.[35]

I think it is no accident that in *Grendel* and *Keywords*, too, we find an anxiety about the encroachments of desire, or that both were written by men who had come of age in farming regions and who had seen these regions undergo radical change in step with the rise of the global supermarket system. In many ways at odds with each other—on the face of it little connects the dissenting definitions of *Keywords* with the Gnostic outpourings of *Grendel*—their visions nonetheless hinge on a single concern, which might in turn seem a central fear among the interested parties of their wartime generation. From cultural contexts otherwise unalike, Williams and Gardner together illuminate a new structure in the feeling of need. They present themselves as agents of history, and they draw upon their long perspective on the past to shed new light on an ontological shift they feel is happening before their eyes, a shift in which sensations of food desire, or hunger, continue to recur, echoing with undimmed force, even as they drift away from their old basis in bodily need. Their works, if read in tandem, might even seem to unmask *hunger* as the true skeuomorph: a word and not a pictogram, to be sure, but one which bridges the ancient and the modern and hides the fundamental rupture between the two.

Many of us know you should never go to the supermarket when you are feeling hungry. The problem with doing so is you can end up spending too much. Unless you can exercise restraint, your cart will start to overflow, filling up with unwise impulse buys, not just for now but for several days to come. But to amass such foods against the sudden hunger pangs of the future might also seem paradoxical: a plan for what would happen if there was no plan, or proof that we do not just succumb to suboptimal snacks on the spur of the moment but sometimes schedule them in for the week ahead. Such forward planning, in turn, might seem to offer further proof that the semantic field of hunger now harbors such a confusing mixture of psychological and physical meanings as to confirm that it has indeed become a kind of lexical reply to the visual or iconographic phenomenon of the skeuomorph. Even as it remains a powerful signifier in common speech, hunger's capaciousness now encompasses multiple oppositions. Because post-1945 visions of a future "without starvation" remain unfulfilled, it must continue to denote "genuine" need, and in many contexts it must remain strong enough to "pierce stone walls," as the all-but-forgotten English phrase once had it.[36] But soon it veers into the opposite of this, too, and can as quickly denote an altogether different order of desire, one which has little to do with the body, little to do with gauntness or emaciation or famine or want, and which involves instead what Kent C. Berridge calls "'Wanting' and 'liking'" among other impulses "actively generated by neural systems that paint the desire or pleasure onto the sensation" of food, "a sort of gloss painted on . . . sight, smell or taste," where "sweetness and creaminess are keys that potently unlock the generating brain circuits which apply pleasure and desire to the food at the moment of encounter."[37] The inexorable biopsychological movement toward a neural "liking" or "wanting" of food that is charted in Berridge's work thus seems coincident not only with the global rise of the supermarket but also with the shift Williams identifies from the use-based orientations of the *customer* to the destructions left in the wake of the *consumer*. It too charts our movement into a new mode of individual engagement no longer predicated on need or use but on the duty to consume, and indeed to make our identities through that consumption, and to do so by consuming "what industry finds it convenient to produce."[38] It too recasts the stomach, placing it behind a cart that becomes its external echo, understanding the two as a platform for individual identity formation and a place to deposit waste both edible (stomach) and inedible (cart).

Obesity, however, does offer us visual proof of this waste, reminding us of our undue reliance on the natural resources of the world. In Pixar's ninth film, *WALL-E* (2008), the human escapees of a dead beige world grow soft and lose bone density as they wait around in the microgravity environment of the *Axiom*, their gargantuan spaceship. Some on board seem happy to sink into the carts that carry them from one leisure space to another. But *WALL-E* makes it clear that all who live this life of pure convenience are now regressing to an infantile state in which they are dependent and without restraint. The probe robots that the *Axiom* sends to earth in search of returning plant life might create clear parallels with the reconnoitering doves of Noah's ark—parallels which, as Eric Herhuth notes, have encouraged a groundswell of Christian enthusiasm for the film.[39] But the analogy also draws attention to the fact that unlike Noah or his animals, the occupants of this interplanetary ark are themselves degenerate and share with their destroyed planet a need to regain lost vitality and vigor. Indeed, if the Disney logo before *WALL-E*'s opening credits had already led us to expect that the film would offer us an exercise in moral education, then the sight of these obese (but perfect) bodies now suggests what this lesson might be. From this point forward, certainly, anyone with a passing knowledge of Hollywood melodrama can anticipate that the human souls buried inside these fat bodies will soon wake up to the deadening impact of their lives of pleasure. A little mild peril will follow this awakening, but triumph will then ensue, and when it does so it will take the form of a renewed communion between them and the natural world that some earlier incarnation of humanity destroyed. Lapsarianism, reversible, will spark the regreening of their lost beige world; the world will forgive them and become Edenic again.

It is hard not to feel that the future that is now heading in our direction will follow a different trajectory. In some ways, the leading multinational corporations of the industrial food system are already beginning to display greater ethical responsibility toward the anthropocentric exception that is the human body. Nutritional food, for some, is becoming easier to find, and in US policy discussions of the food desert the introduction of supermarkets is often invoked as the obvious solution to health problems associated with a fast-food diet. Some of these developments seem likely to continue. The global supermarket system might soon learn to do without the cart, and it might even become less reliant on sugar, meat, and salt, reorienting the continents under its control toward the production of the salad leaves and whole grains that we now associate with a healthier life. Even overconsumers might lose weight; the foods of the supermarket might simply evaporate as they enter our orbits, burning up in an atmosphere of dietary self-flagellation and ritualized gym pain. But even hair-shirt consumerism is excessive if it operates under what Lewis Mumford long ago characterized as a "capitalist" mode of "extraction" which confuses "ownership" of the land with its "security of tenure" and continues to strip it of mineral wealth.[40] For the car and the fridge remain "for the most part tethered to a netherworld of rocks and reservoirs," as Gavin Bridge has suggested, and even when what they carry is low in fat and high in vitamins.[41] A carton of strawberries in the middle of a northern winter need not cause your stomach to inflate, but it probably carries a higher environmental cost than some of the supermarket's sugary and salty dry goods. The history of the cart that I have traced in this essay has also been a history of the ugly feelings the cart has always attracted. It has shown that the cart has offered the people a solution which the people have then seen as a problem in turn. But at least these disliked carts have shown up on the radar of overconsumption. At least, like the obese bodies which US culture holds in similar contempt, they have helped to explain or at least indicate that globalization is happening. The risk now is that if carts do indeed disappear and obesity rates begin to reduce, we forget what Warren Belasco calls the "domino" or "downstream" impact of all that we consume.[42] No one can calculate the consequences of such invisible excess; no one can afford to ignore the planet inside us all.

NOTES

ENTRANCE

1. Goldman Sachs report, "Totally Addicted to Space: Overcapacity in UK Grocery Still Needs to Be Addressed," 5. Accessed 28 September 2017 at www.thegrocer.co.uk/download.aspx.
2. Deborah Orr, "The UK's Big Supermarkets Sowed the Seeds of Their Own Decline," *Guardian*, Friday, 3 October 2014. www.theguardian.com/commentisfree/2014/oct/03/uk-big-supermarkets-sowed-seeds-own-decline
3. Ryne Misso, "Amazon's Growth into Private Label Should Put Grocers on High Alert," *Progressive Grocer*, August 2016. www.nexis.com/results/enhdocview.do
4. "Shopper's Delight," *Life*, 3 January 1955, 38–39. https://books.google.co.uk/books
5. "A Triumph and an Obligation" (editorial), *Life*, 3 January 1955, 2–3. https://books.google.co.uk/books
6. For a summation of Potter's thesis, see "Abundance and the Shaping of American Character," in *People of Plenty*, 73–77. Although originally published in 1953, *People of Plenty* was based on the patriotic Walgreen Foundation lectures Potter had given at the University of Chicago in 1950.

7. "What's Ahead for Supermarket Shoppers," *Changing Times,* November 1958. https://books.google.co.uk/books

8. Nora, "Between Memory and History," 18.

9. Jeffrey D. Zbar, "Speed & Ease Drive Store of the Future; Package Goods to Come from On-Line Service as Grocery to Focus on Fresh Food," *Advertising Age,* 2 May 1994. www.nexis.com/results/enhdocview.do. See also Belasco, *Meals to Come,* 242–43.

10. Lorrie Grant, "Grocery Chore No More: Time-Strapped Shoppers Buy On-Line, Get Goods Delivered to Their Doors," *USA Today,* 21 July 1999. www.nexis.com/results/enhdocview.do

11. Mary Dejevsky, "Totally Bananas; Why Did George Shaheen, The Big Cheese at Andersen Consulting, Give It All Up for Webvan. A Small-Potatoes, Online, Grocery Delivery Service?" *Independent,* 10 November 1999. www.nexis.com/results/enhdocview.do

12. Chris Partridge, "You've Got the Order—Now Deliver," *London Times,* 24 March 2000. www.nexis.com/results/enhdocview.do

13. For example, the inventor of the safety razor, King Gillette, and the inventor of the revolving door, Theophilus Van Kannel, are included in the National Inventors Hall of Fame. Accessed 16 December 2016 at www.nndb.com/honors/032/000111696/.

14. A possible exception here is Julian Montague, author of the conversation piece *The Stray Shopping Carts of Eastern North America: A Guide to Field Identification.*

15. Will Self, "Soon Our Personalities Will Be Purely Ornamental," *New Statesman,* 10 October 2013. www.newstatesman.com/consumer-tech/2013/10/skeuomorphs-are-taking-over-soon-our-personalities-will-be-purely-ornamental. On the etymology of *skeuomorph,* see Blitz, "Skeuomorphs, Pottery, and Technological Change."

16. *Oxford English Dictionary.* Accessed 23 December 2016 at http://o-www.oed.com.wam.leeds.ac.uk/view/Entry/180780.

17. Hilary Greenbaum and Dana Rubenstein, "Grocery Shopping on Speed," *New York Times,* 16 December 2011. www.nytimes.com/2011/12/18/magazine/who-made-that-shopping-cart.html

18. As the archaeologist Blitz notes in his study of pre-Columbian baskets and potsherds: "Encounters with unfamiliar innovations trigger different emotional responses. . . . As change is accommodated,

some people may not want the same old objects, but others do not wish to relinquish the associated positive emotions. Within the social group, skeuomorphs are part of the social process that resolves this innovation dilemma. The signifying quality of skeuomorphs fosters acceptance of technology by ... evoking positive memories of familiar experiences associated with the prototype." Blitz, "Skeuomorphs, Pottery, and Technological Change," 673.

19. Cubitt, "Distribution and Media Flows," 200.
20. Bob Ingram, "Wheels of Fortune," *Progressive Grocer*, 1 January 2012. https://progressivegrocer.com/wheels-fortune
21. Yannig Roth, "The IDEO Shopping Cart (1998) Wasn't a Failure, the Concept Was Just Ahead of Its Time." Accessed 28 September 2017 at https://yannigroth.com/2011/08/12/the-ideo-shopping-cart-1998-wasnt-a-failure-the-concept-was-just-ahead-of-its-time/.
22. Bob Ingram, "Wheels of Fortune," *Progressive Grocer*, 1 January 2012. https://progressivegrocer.com/wheels-fortune
23. Carlo Ratti, *Supermarket of the Future,* World Expo 2015 Milan. Accessed 28 September 2017 at www.carloratti.com/project/supermarket-of-the-future/.
24. Han, *Transparency Society*, 13.
25. For an examination of the important semantic distinction between "modulation" and older notions of "versions" and "copies," see Shaviro, *Post-Cinematic Affect*,13–14.
26. Brown, "Neoliberalism, Neoconservatism, and De-Democratization," 694. Emphasis in original.
27. Han, *In the Swarm*, 67.
28. Fisher, *Capitalist Realism*, 70.
29. Cochoy and Grandclément-Chaffy, "Publicizing Goldilocks' Choice at the Supermarket," 652–53.
30. Alworth, *Site Reading,* 39.
31. Deutsch, *Building a Housewife's Paradise,* 22.

CHAPTER 1. INSIDE VIEWS

1. The quotation is from the informal history offered on the website of the Piggly Wiggly supermarket chain. Accessed 28 September

2017 at http://idigthepig.com/about-our-store. The case of the sixty-two-year-old Englishwoman Eliza Carroll is instructive here. Her conviction for theft in 1962 came about after she had used "two shopping bags" during her visit to a new local self-service store, "but only paid for the contents of one when she reached the cash desk." Her mitigation on the grounds of confusion was accepted by the magistrate insofar as he agreed that such new stores were "a menace and a scourge," explaining that "everyone who goes into them is under suspicion. There have been more larceny cases in this court than ever before because of them. It's so easy." Similar cases, and similar fears over the new opportunities for shoplifting that self-service shopping afforded, soon followed the establishment of supermarkets in many other cultural contexts. The introduction of the cart offered a means of reducing such opportunities and also helped prevent the likes of Carroll from falling into crime inadvertently. But it did so, arguably, at the cost of entrenching further the "suspicion" built into the structure of the new self-service store, forcing all to make their choices visible to all and trusting no one with their own bags. "Self-Service Stores 'a Menace,'" *Guardian*, 20 March 1962. www.lexisnexis.com/en-us/products/nexis.page

    2. Wells, *Car Country*, 289.

    3. Flaubert, *Madame Bovary*, 67.

    4. Gaskell, *Sylvia's Lovers*, 24.

    5. An important exception here is Emile Zola's *The Ladies' Paradise*, which Bill Brown describes as "the first novelistic treatment of the department store," and as a clear European forerunner of Dreiser's *Sister Carrie*. Brown, *Sense of Things*, 32.

    6. Dreiser, *Sister Carrie*, 20.

    7. Bowlby, *Just Looking*, 36.

    8. Bowlby, *Just Looking*, 4; Friedberg, *Window Shopping*, 42. My argument here thus also takes issue with that of James B. Twitchell's *Living It Up: Our Love Affair with Luxury*, which similarly cites this passage from the novel before suggesting that Carrie here "passes a department store window" and "Dreiser describes what she sees." The transformative, epochal significance that scholars frequently find in the

passage hinges on the fact that Carrie goes inside. Twitchell, *Living It Up*, 81.

9. Bowlby, *Just Looking*, 19. As Adam Mack puts it, Bowlby and other cultural historians have often "emphasized visual spectacle as the dominant expressive mode" of commodity consumerism, often overlooking the part played by the "other four senses in creating a society organized around getting and spending." Mack, "'Speaking of Tomatoes,'" 816.

10. "Elaborate but Smooth-Working Machinery," *New York Times*, 11 December 1904, SM1. https://o-search-proquest-com.wam.leeds.ac.uk/hnpnewyorktimes/news/fromDatabasesLayer

11. Brown, *Sense of Things*, 32–33.

12. Barry, *Bon Marché*, 165. A complication here lies in the fact that The Fair Store's founder Ernst J. Lehmann always insisted it would offer "many different things for sale at a cheap price," acquiring a reputation as a discount store; see Ledermann, *Christmas on State Street*, 33. This real-life store's focus on affordability ebbs away from *Sister Carrie*, eclipsed by its emphasis on the "dainty" and "delicate" goods; in turn, in an early example of Dreiser's anti-Semitism, "a sharp, quick-mannered Jew," perhaps an unnamed version of Lehmann, appears from behind the scenes before determining of Carrie, "we can't use you." Dreiser, *Sister Carrie*, 21.

13. Dreiser, *Sister Carrie*, 21.

14. Dreiser, Sister Carrie, 21.

15. The narrative scheme of Henry James's *The Golden Bowl* (1904) depends on a similar interest in the new tactile pleasures of modern city shopping. James's lingering description of the "slim light fingers, with neat nails," of the Bloomsbury shopkeeper who first hands the eponymous bowl to Charlotte Stant establishes it from the start as a tactile object rather than an ornament. As other hands are then seen holding, weighing, and smashing it, James's novel confirms the multisensory focus of Dreiser's realist *Sister Carrie*. James, *Golden Bowl*, 103.

16. Longstreth, *Drive-In, The Supermarket, and the Transformation of Commercial Space in Los Angeles, 1914–1941*, xiiv.

17. Michaels, "*Sister Carrie*'s Popular Economy," 382–83.

CHAPTER 2. ARISTOCRATIC BASKETS

1. Quoted in Bowlby, *Carried Away*, 140.
2. Longstreth, *Drive-In, the Supermarket, and the Transformation of Commercial Space in Los Angeles, 1914–1941*, xiv.
3. Hyman, *Debtor Nation*, 11–12. As Hyman suggests, the new importance of "instalment credit allowed consumers to buy more, retailers to sell more, and manufacturers to make more.... Personal loans, meanwhile, enabled those industrial workers who made all these goods to weather the uncertainties of capitalism's labor market.... Retailers, perhaps, experienced the greatest transformation as debt became resellable." Hyman thus effectively suggests that as credit underwent reorganization after World War One, becoming a source of new profits, its visibility at once faded from local stores—where it had always been understood as a "convenience" to the individual customer—and became more important to their actual sales.
4. *Progressive Grocer* editor Carl Dipman discusses "talking signs" at length in his 1931 manual *The Modern Grocery Store*, but his coinage only confirms an advertising phenomenon already apparent in the coordinated campaigns which Kellogg's and other grocery product businesses launched in the 1910s and early 1920s. Dipman, *Modern Grocery Store*, 139.
5. Tolbert, "Beyond Piggly Wiggly," 6–8. As the *New York Times* reported in 1919, "The increased cost of clerk hire and the scarcity of store help have caused quite a few merchants to introduce self-service departments." "Devices in Use for Self-Selling," *New York Times*, 19 October 1919, E10. https://o-search-proquest-com.wam.leeds.ac.uk/hnpnewyorktimes/news/fromDatabasesLayer
6. Surdam, *Century of the Leisured Masses*, 46.
7. As Susan Benson suggests, "managers persistently attacked" the "collective aspects" of department store saleswomen's working lives. "They tried to take over saleswomen's shop-floor wisdom and to break the power of their work groups," and they also "tried to co-opt saleswomen's collectively devised selling secrets." Benson, "Customers Ain't God," 200. Annelise Orleck adds that a fault line between the Women's Trade Union League and its sister organization, the National

Women's Party, opened up in 1923 after "one Washington department store cut saleswomen's wages by 50 percent." Orleck, *Common Sense and a Little Fire*, 140.

8. Benson, "Customers Ain't God," 193.
9. Benson, "Customers Ain't God," 196.
10. Barthes, "New Citroën," 90.
11. Tolbert, "Beyond Piggly Wiggly," 9.
12. Longstreth, *Department Store Transformed, 1920–1960*, 1–3.
13. "A Self-Service Grocery," *New York Times*, 23 December 1917, 40. https://o-search-proquest-com.wam.leeds.ac.uk/hnpnewyorktimes/news/fromDatabasesLayer
14. Martin and Hansen, *Newspapers of Record in a Digital Age*, 7.
15. Deutsch, *Building a Housewife's Paradise*, 26.
16. Freidberg, *Fresh*, 44–47.
17. By the 1950s, as Packard observed, "less than one shopper in five" would have a complete list, "but still the wives always manage to fill up their carts." Packard *Hidden Persuaders*, 112.
18. Fearing a rise in shoplifting was a common response to the shift to self-service. The opening of the first department of all, Paris Le Bon Marché, generated acute concern over a new condition known as kleptomania. http://o-quod.lib.umich.edu.wam.leeds.ac.uk/cgi/t/text/pageviewer-idx. By 1953, in a confidential employee manual for Acme Supermarkets, the firm's vice president agreed, observing that "shoplifters never had it so good as they have since food merchants introduced the self-service system." Johnson, *Shoplifter Racket*, 2. Longstreth suggests such fears tended to overstate the problem, at least in the context of the US department store. Longstreth, *Department Store Transformed, 1920–1960*, 35.
19. Halper, *Shopping Center and Store Leases*, 114.
20. Quoted in Tolbert, "Aristocracy of the Market Basket," 187.
21. Belasco, *Meals to Come*, 174.
22. Saunders, *Self-Serving Store*. US1242872. 21 October 1916. www.google.co.uk/patents/US1242872. As Longstreth comments, later interwar developments would lead department stores and supermarkets away from using their front or street windows as "a means of displaying produce." Such traditional "frontality," however, remains a

key concern of Saunders's patent and even leads him to stipulate that such fridge displays be situated so that they can be seen "from the side-walk immediately in front of the store." Longstreth, *Drive-In, the Supermarket, and the Transformation of Commercial Space in Los Angeles, 1914–1941*, 109–10.

23. Quoted in Tolbert, "Aristocracy of the Market Basket," 191.

24. Quoted in Freeman, *Clarence Saunders and the Founding of Piggly Wiggly*, 27.

25. Tolbert, "Aristocracy of the Market Basket," 181.

26. Abel, "Bathroom Doors and Drinking Fountains," 441.

27. The ad may be found at www.periodpaper.com/collections/corporate-business-general/products/1929-ad-piggly-wiggly-grocery-stores-shopping-food-roaring-twenties-fashion-ygh2-228313-ygh2-044.

28. Tolbert, "Aristocracy of the Market Basket," 183.

29. Tolbert, "Beyond Piggly Wiggly," 26.

30. Abel, "American Graffiti," 11. See also Hale, *Making Whiteness*, 186.

31. Tolbert, "Aristocracy of the Market Basket," 193.

32. Hale, *Making Whiteness*, 193.

33. Hale, *Making Whiteness*, 164.

34. Veblen, *Theory of the Leisure Class*, 90.

35. Bordo, *Unbearable Weight*, 125.

36. Bordo, *Unbearable Weight*, 100.

37. "Piggly Wiggly for Antipodes," *New York Times*, 23 August 1928. https://search.proquest.com/hnpnewyorktimes/docview/104483655/19C13D0A9EAE441FPQ/59. On the adoption of *All over the World* as a slogan, see Freeman, *Clarence Saunders and the Founding of Piggly Wiggly*, 36.

38. Mayo's assessment is that "Saunders accepted racial prejudice and segregation, as did most people at the time. But strident, ugly anti-black statements were an aberration for him." Mayo, *American Grocery Store*, 109.

39. Ferris, *Edible South*, 193. See also Freeman, *Clarence Saunders and the Founding of Piggly Wiggly*, 36.

40. Bowlby, *Carried Away*, 143.

41. See "About King Kullen Supermarkets." Accessed on 28 September 2017 at www.kingkullen.com/about-us/.

42. Clark, *Fitch's List of Super-Markets*, iii. See also Longstreth, *Drive-In, the Supermarket, and the Transformation of Commercial Space in Los Angeles, 1914–1941*, 78.

43. Zimmerman, "Supermarket and the Changing Retail Structure," 403.

44. See "About King Kullen Supermarkets." Accessed on 28 September 2017 at www.kingkullen.com/about-us/.

45. Halper suggests that in the years before his death Cullen increasingly stood out among his competitors because he "didn't expect to provide or pay for an adjacent parking lot." Halper, *Shopping Center and Store Leases*, 39.

46. Quotation, albeit of familiar terminology, is from Mumford, *City in History*, 576. Although King Kullen's own website suggests that the chain only expanded into Long Island during the 1950s, several branch stores in Suffolk and Nassau Counties are listed in *The Long-Islander*, 25 July 1940, 7. http://nyshistoricnewspapers.org/lccn/sn83031119/1940-07-25

47. National Cash Register Company, "Suggestions to Merchants" (undated and unattributed). Saunders had provided an early taste of such car-centered language as far back as the 1910s. His newspaper ad of 1916 promised readers that changes "in the checking system ... will relieve ... congestion," allowing "you to get by ... without any 'jamming' of folks behind you." Freeman, *Clarence Saunders and the Founding of Piggly Wiggly*, 35.

48. Belasco, *Meals to Come*, 174.

49. Berman, *All That Is Solid Melts into Air*, 308. On the economic history of 1930s roadbuilding, see Field, "Economic Growth and Recovery in the United States, 1919–1941," 361.

50. Halper, *Shopping Center and Store Leases*, 127. I follow Halper here in finding the analogy of car and cart more historically apposite than James Mayo's earlier comparison of the latter with a rail freight car. Mayo, *American Grocery Store*, 150.

51. Longstreth, *Drive-In, the Supermarket, and the Transformation of Commercial Space*, 38.

52. Longstreth suggests that "out of an estimate 350 Los Angeles supermarkets built by 1939, only about 40 percent were yielding the handsome profits that had lured so many merchants into the fray." Longstreth, *Drive-In, the Supermarket, and the Transformation of Commercial Space*, 111.

CHAPTER 3. IN THE SUPERMARKET

1. Lefebvre, *Critique of Everyday Life*, 97.
2. Latour, Harman, and Erdélyi, *Prince and the Wolf*, 33.
3. Latour, *We Have Never Been Modern*, 14.
4. Nojeim, *Gandhi and King*, 17.
5. Bennett, *Vibrant Matter*, 120.
6. Latour, *Reassembling the Social*, 64.
7. Latour, *Reassembling the Social*, 209–10. Emphases in original.
8. Katti and Latour, "Mediating Political 'Things,' and the Forked Tongue of Modern Culture," 110.
9. Alworth, *Site Reading*, 29.
10. Agamben, *Infancy and History*, 13–14. Baudrillard, *Consumer Society*, 110. For reasons he leaves unexplained, Baudrillard describes the supermarket as "that great shoppers' funeral parlour" in *America*, 30–31.
11. In *The Last Testament: The Making of 'London Calling,'* a documentary video released to coincide with the twenty-fifth anniversary edition of *London Calling* in 2004, Strummer said he wrote the lyrics imagining Jones's life growing up in a basement with his mother and grandmother.
12. Horkheimer and Adorno, *Dialectic of Enlightenment*, 168. See also Fromm, *Escape from Freedom*, 75.
13. In this, the supermarket might, for them, signify what Mark Fisher called "the *negative atheology* proper to Capital," in which "the centre is missing, but we cannot stop searching for it." See *Capitalist Realism*, 65.
14. Augé, *Non-Places*, 78.
15. Cochoy, "Driving a Shopping Cart from STS to Business, and the Other Way Round," 32; Miller, *Theory of Shopping*, 33.
16. Norris, *Pit*, 80.

17. *Crop Production Historical Track Records*, 207. Accessed 28 September 2017 at http://usda.mannlib.cornell.edu/usda/current/htrcp/htrcp-04-13-2017.pdf.

18. Mintz, *Sweetness and Power*, 148.

19. *Crop Production Historical Track Records*, 207. Accessed 28 September 2017 at http://usda.mannlib.cornell.edu/usda/current/htrcp/htrcp-04-13-2017.pdf.

20. Quotation is from *Now a Modern Foodstore: As Easy as ABC* (1938), 2–3, the trade catalogue of Lyon Metal Products, Inc., supplier of "open, accessible" shelving.

21. Wik, "Review of Fordson, Farmall, and Poppin' Johnny," 626. For an account of technological change in the Depression era with a focus on its new inventions and on its success in popularizing old ones, see Field, "Economic Growth and Recovery in the United States, 1919–1941," 360–61. Further consideration of the contemporary developments in refrigeration in domestic use and in rail and road transportation appears in Tressler, *Freezing Preservation of Fruits, Juices and Vegetables*, 261; and Freidberg, *Fresh*, 184. The rise in malnutrition during this period corresponds to Amartya Sen's well-known demonstration in the early 1980s that malnutrition and famine result from a collapse not in production but in income. Sen, *Poverty and Famines*, 155.

22. For a case study detailing the particularities of this process in the case of UK supermarket chicken, see Jackson, *Anxious Appetites*, 68.

23. Boyd and Watts consider the adaptation of JIT (which had originated in the Japanese car industry) to "biological" and "agrarian" systems of food production and transportation in the postwar US. Boyd and Watts, "Agro-Industrial Just in Time," 149–51.

24. See, for example, the portrait of the commercial tactics of Gordon Corbaley, interwar president of the American Institute of Food Distribution, in Zimmerman's *Super Market: A Revolution in Distribution*, 13. For the history of such integration with specific reference to the US supermarket and chicken supplies, see Boyd and Watts "Agro-Industrial Just in Time," 149–51.

25. Longstreth, *Drive-In, the Supermarket, and the Transformation of Commercial Space in Los Angeles, 1914–1941*, 121. Halper, *Shopping Center and*

Store Leases, 39. Carl W. Dipman, "The Self-Service Store—Things to Do in Planning," *Progressive Grocer,* November 1937, 71.

26. Deutsch, *Building a Housewife's Paradise,* 43.
27. Dipman, *Modern Grocery Store,* v.
28. Dipman, *Modern Grocery Store,* 34.
29. Dipman, *Modern Grocery Store,* iv.
30. Although the ultimate results of such debates remain inconclusive, ongoing research into the relative virtues of "clockwise" and "counterclockwise" floor plans often registers similar surprise on discovering that, in the supermarket, the fastest flow of goods often occurs when customers slow down; one study in Japan demonstrated that "clockwise" customers spend significantly more because they are "not efficient," taking a longer route around the store. Kholod, Takai and Yada, "Clockwise and Anti-clockwise Directions of Customer Orientation in a Supermarket," 308.
31. Dipman, *Modern Grocery Store,* v.
32. Dipman, *Modern Grocery Store,* 8.

CHAPTER 4. THE LATE CART

1. As Freidberg suggests, the "shifts in seasonal supply became less pronounced ... by the end of the 1930s. Freidberg, *Fresh,* 47.
2. Freidberg, *Fresh,* 45. On Hussmann's first open or self-service freezer cabinet, see www.hussmann.com/en/About-Us/Pages/Historical-Overview.aspx. For a full and interesting contemporary account of developments in commercial refrigeration earlier in the decade, see Tressler, *Freezing Preservation of Fruits, Juices and Vegetables,* 267–77. See also McAusland, *Supermarkets,* 42.
3. "Wrapping Machines for Economy, Appearance and Protection." Package Machinery Company Trade catalogue (1934).
4. Quoted in "Sylvan N. Goldman Dies; Inventor of the Shopping Cart," *New York Times,* 27 November 1984, B7. https://o-search-proquest-com.wam.leeds.ac.uk/hnpnewyorktimes/docview/122410254/E0BAA9F743CF4348PQ/1

5. Grandclément, *Wheeling Food Products around the Store... and Away*, 7. Grandclément notes that other supermarkets at the time also experimented with this simple human solution.

6. Halper, *Shopping Center and Store Leases*, 82.

7. Tolbert, "Aristocracy of the Market Basket," 182–92. On Ralph's Grocery Stores' movement away from home delivery in Los Angeles, see Halper, *Shopping Center and Store Leases*, 103.

8. David Nye lists key uses of the phrase "technological sublime"—ultimately tracing it back to Perry Miller's *Life of the Mind in America*—in his *American Technological Sublime*, xv. For his discussion of the public reaction to the Hoover Dam's opening, see *American Technological Sublime*, 137–40.

9. Weingarten is cited as Goldman's chief precursor in Grandclément, *Wheeling Food Products around the Store... and Away*, 9–10. In the 1910s, as Grandclément suggests, "Weingarten had invented a basket-carrier from a toy wagon and had improved it, so that... he was attributed with the introduction of the basket-carrier" in Zimmerman's 1955 work *The Super Market: A Revolution in Distribution*, 26–28. Longstreth includes Houston in his short list of locations where the "most significant prototypes" for the American supermarket "existed" before about 1940 (the other two are Southern California and suburban New York). Longstreth, *Drive-In, the Supermarket, and the Transformation of Commercial Space in Los Angeles, 1914–1941*, 121.

10. Field, "Most Technologically Progressive Decade of the Century," 1405.

11. Steinbeck, *Sweet Thursday*, 194.

12. Field notes that car ownership increased as rates of production stayed steady while many of the vehicles produced in the 1920s remained on the road. Field, "Most Technologically Progressive Decade of the Century," 1405.

13. Mumford, *Culture of Cities*, 495.

14. Mumford, *Technics and Civilization*, 79–80.

15. Apparently unaware of his earlier career, Zimmerman dismisses Young as Goldman's "carpenter" in *The Super Market*, 152.

16. Goldman, *Combination Basket and Carriage*, US2155896. 4 May 1937. www.google.com/patents/US2155896

17. Grandclément, *Wheeling Food Products around the Store ... and Away*, 7.

18. Goldman, *Folding Basket Carriage for Self-Service Stores*, US2196914. 14 March 1938. www.google.com/patents/US2196914. On the importance of Young's contribution, see also Halper, *Shopping Center and Store Leases*, 125–26.

19. Grandclément, *Wheeling Food Products around the Store ... and Away*, 3.

20. McAusland, *Supermarkets*, 65.

21. Jackson, *Hangsaman*, 181. Ginsberg, *Howl and Other Poems*, 24.

22. Advertisement in the *Oklahoma City Times*, 4 June 1937, quoted in Wilson, *Cart That Changed the World*, 84.

23. Grandclément, *Wheeling Food Products around the Store ... and Away*, 6.

24. Halper, *Shopping Center and Store Leases*, 49.

25. Wilson, *Cart That Changed the World*, 88.

26. Zimmerman, *Super Market*, 153.

27. Wilson, *Cart That Changed the World*, 89.

28. For a useful discussion on US cultural views of the child consumer, see Daniel Cook, "Disempowering Empowerment of Children's Consumer 'Choice,'" 42–43. Malene Gram provides an interesting counterpoint to long-standing US debate in her study of the "help" and "self-regulating" influence children offer their families when supermarket shopping in Denmark. Gram, "Supermarket Revisited," 40.

29. Cochoy, "Driving a Shopping Cart from STS to Business, and the Other Way Round," 48–49.

30. Grandclément, *Wheeling Food Products around the Store ... and Away*, 7.

31. Mussell, *Science, Time and Space in the Late Nineteenth Century Periodical Press*, 50.

32. As Milton Friedman, for one, declared, "there are many 'inventions' that are not patentable. The 'inventor' of the supermarket, for example, conferred great benefits on his fellowmen for which he could not charge them." Friedman, *Capitalism and Freedom*, 127.

33. Saunders, *Self-Serving Store*. US1242872. 21 October 1916. www.google.co.uk/patents/US1242872

34. Quotation is from the wall of history at Nashville's Bicentennial Capitol Mall. http://tnstateparks.com/parks/about/bicentennial-mall

35. Grandclément, *Wheeling Food Products around the Store ... and Away*, 11.

36. Goldman, *Child Seat for Store Service Carriers*. US2662775A. 15 September 1950. https://patents.google.com/patent/US2662775A/en

37. Grandclément, *Wheeling Food Products around the Store ... and Away*, 15–16.

38. Latour, Harman, and Erdélyi, *Prince and the Wolf*, 75.

39. Wells, *Car Country*, 295.

40. Caro, *Power Broker*, 936.

41. Bivens, "Inequality, Exhibit A."

42. Jameson, *Valences of the Dialectic*, 424.

43. Bennett, *Vibrant Matter*, 50.

44. Finlayson and Dalton, "Hedonics of Food Consumption," 42.

45. A report which Cynthia Ogden and her team at the Centers for Disease Control and Prevention published in 2004 offered a statistical history demonstrating that since 1960, at least, Americans had indeed been getting bigger. Of their sample of American men between twenty and seventy-nine years in 1960, their data showed a mean weight of 75.6 kilograms, whereas that for a similar sample in 1999 was 86.1 kilograms—an increase of 13.9 percent. The weight of American women from the same group rose from a mean of 63.7 kilograms in 1960 to 74.7 kilograms, an increase of 17.3 percent. It seems widely accepted that the chronological range of this data only captures a historical portion of a rise in average body weight which predated 1960 and which continues to the present day. A more statistical approach than my own could readily assemble a bar chart that not only confirmed this historical increase but placed it next to a further dataset showing that it coincided with a similarly steady rise in the supermarket's overall share of the US economy's grocery or food sector. While some might have cried foul at such a juxtaposition, feeling it mistook corre-

lation for causation, the purpose of this cultural history is to argue that the rise in the supermarket cart and the growth of the average body pushing it along are linked, and not just in the United States. See Ogden et al., "Mean Body Weight, Height, and Body Mass Index, United States 1960–2002," 9.

46. Finlayson and Dalton, "Hedonics of Food Consumption," 42.

47. Cheever, "Ocean," 735.

CHAPTER 5. CARTS UNCHAINED

1. Although many at the time dated the Australian adoption of the American supermarket to 1960, and specifically to the opening in that year of an impressively large branch store of Dickens in the Melbourne suburb of Balwyn North, the introduction of such stores and their carts in fact took place early in the 1950s. The opening of Beshara's new "highway supermarket" was announced in the *Adelaide Post* in June 1953, attributing it to a businessman who, like Marks and Spencer's Michael Marks, had recently paid a long research trip to America "studying self-service techniques." His innovation bore the hallmark of Goldman's influence insofar as it aimed to solve the problem of shoppers being "laden with parcels" by providing them with a "shopping cart" complete with an "attachment ... for very young children." "The 'Supermarket' Arrives," *Adelaide Post*, 12 June 1953. At the time of this early development, *Cairns Post* and *The Farmer and Settler* were continuing to provide curious Australian readers with enthusiastic reports of the early successes and new innovations of Clarence Saunders in Tennessee. "Man with Ideas Has One More: Automatic Grocery," *Cairns Post*, 21 September 1953; and "The Customers Do All the Work in This Food Shop," *The Farmer and Settler*, 30 October 1953. Reports from http://trove.nla.gov.au/newspaper/result. The Laurie Richards Collection at the Melbourne Arts Centre includes many documentary photographs of carts in use at Ritchies and other supermarket chains in Melbourne from 1956 onward. http://collections.artscentremelbourne.com.au/paminter/imu.php

2. Information on Goulet-Turpin can be found at www.journaldunet.com/economie/reportage/premier-supermarche/3-le-froid.shtml.

3. Azuchi, *Supermarket*, 66.

4. Dower, *Embracing Defeat*, 209.
5. Deutsch, *Building a Housewife's Paradise*, p.191.
6. "The Market of Mr Mikoyan," *Le Monde*, 8 January 1959. www.lemonde.fr/archives/article/1959/01/08/le-marche-de-m-mikoyan_2168646_1819218.html#1t8g5jd3gzRsbo6M.99
7. George Kitchen, "Queen Visits U.S. Supermarket, Surprises Saturday Food Shoppers," *Saskatoon Star-Phoenix*, 21 October 1957. https://news.google.com/newspapers
8. Spufford, *Red Plenty*, 22.
9. On the modernistic design of postwar supermarkets, see Belasco, *Meals to Come*, 175.
10. "Converted Loft Space," *Forum: Magazine of Building*, January 1962.
11. Dorothy Diamond, "The Woman's Viewpoint," *Printers' Ink: The Weekly Magazine of Advertising and Marketing*, 29 April 1960.
12. Walter Landor, "Consumer Research Part of Packaging Design," *Food Field Reporter*, 12 September 1960.
13. Walter Landor, "Industrial Design Is Part of Advertising," *Western Advertising*, February 1948, 56.
14. "All Products Should 'Smile,' Says Expert on Packaging," *Seattle Times*, 22 November 1955.
15. Bowlby, *Carried Away*, 163.
16. "Best Seller Now Sells Even Better," *Good Packaging*, April 1955.
17. "A New V8 Hits the Road," *Packaging Digest*, undated.
18. Palley, "Economics and Political Economy of Milton Friedman," 635.
19. Robin, *Reactionary Mind*, 88.
20. The full text of "A Future That Works," Ronald Reagan's speech to the Conservative Political Action Committee in 1987, can be found at the comprehensive website RonaldReagan2020.US. Accessed on 29 September 2017 at http://reagan2020.us/speeches/A_Future_That_Works.asp.
21. Benjamin, "One-Way Street," 62.
22. Quoted in Benjamin, "Work of Art in the Age of Mechanical Reproduction," 231.
23. Žižek in *Pervert's Guide to Ideology* (2012).

EXIT

1. Chance meetings occur in anonymous supermarket aisles in a range of films from *Ipcress File* (1965) to *The Big Sick* (2017). A TV equivalent of this scene occurs in "Wanna Partner?" *The Good Wife*, Episode 22, Season 6 (2015).
2. DeLillo, *Americana*, 206.
3. Elkin, *The Franchiser*, 1–3.
4. Hall, *One Day*, 24.
5. McDaniels, "Supermarket Blues."
6. Elkin, *Franchiser*, 103.
7. Williams, *Towards 2000*, 188.
8. Gilroy, *Darker than Blue*, 24.
9. Augé, *Non-Places*, 78.
10. Kracaeur, *Mass Ornament*, 76.
11. Bachelard, *Poetics of Space*, 125.
12. Stephen Groening is here writing about the mobile phone, which he characterizes as a "shield" that insulates us from "unwanted contact" as "the hyperstimulus of modern urban environments." The cigarette and its associated paraphernalia might offer another example of such a shield, the protective capacities that they offer to smokers being a neglected social factor in leading accounts of surmounting tobacco addiction. Groening, "From 'A box in the Theatre of the World' to the 'World as Your Living Room,'" 1335.
13. Urry, "Inhabiting the Car," 21.
14. Lefebvre, *Critique of Everyday Life*, 171.
15. Adorno, *Minima Moralia*, 162.
16. *Beowulf*, 4.
17. Gardner, *Grendel*, 31.
18. Gardner, *Grendel*, 37–39.
19. Jameson, *Valences of the Dialectic*, 424.
20. Hardt and Negri, *Empire*, 272; Elkin, *Franchiser*, 3.
21. Shaviro, "Capitalist Monsters," 281.
22. Gardner, *Grendel*, 79.
23. Gardner, *Grendel*, 18.
24. Gardner, *Grendel*, 33–34.

25. Williams, *Long Revolution*, 323.
26. Williams, *Long Revolution*, 323.
27. Williams, *Keywords*, 14.
28. Žižek in *Pervert's Guide to Ideology* (2012).
29. McCarthy, *Road*, 19.
30. McCarthy, *Road*, 34.
31. Lordon, *Willing Slaves of Capitalism*, 49.
32. As Jeremy Davies puts it, the twentieth-century "transformation in regimes of production, consumption, and energy flow constitutes the reshaping of the Holocene epoch into something else: the ongoing birth of the Anthropocene." Davies, *Birth of the Anthropocene*, 187.
33. Further information can be found through the following campaigns: "Slavery in Supply Chains," Anti-Slavery, www.antislavery.org/; "Sugarcane Farming's Toll on the Environment," World Wildlife Fund, www.worldwildlife.org/magazine/issues/summer-2015/articles/sugarcane-farming-s-toll-on-the-environment; and Plastic Oceans, www.plasticoceans.org/.
34. McCarthy, *Road*, 68.
35. On odor in the supermarket, see Mack, "'Speaking of Tomatoes,'" 828.
36. This piece of hyperbole is spoken by Marcus in the opening scene of *Coriolanus*, although Shakespeare also attributes it to the same storehouse of proverbs which holds that "dogs must eat," "meat was made for mouths," and "the gods sent not / corn for the rich men only." *Coriolanus*, 1:1, 203–6. The *Oxford English Dictionary* traces the phrase to English rather than Latin tradition, and specifically to the 1546 work *The Proverbs of John Heywood*, 82.
37. Berridge, Ho, Richard, and DiFeliceantonio, "The Tempted Brain Eats," 44.
38. As Zygmunt Bauman puts it, identity is now "market supplied… . The work dedicated to the construction of identities fit for public display… requires primarily shopping skills." Bauman, *Consuming Life*, 112.
39. Herhuth, "Life, Love, and Programming," 55.
40. Mumford, *Technics and Civilization*, 381f.
41. Bridge, "Hole World," no pagination.
42. Belasco, "How Much Depends on Dinner," 14.

ACKNOWLEDGMENTS

This small book owes many debts. All its errors are mine, but whatever this book achieves is only possible thanks to the support of a wide group of librarians and scholars. A grant from the Leeds Humanities Research Institute enabled me to run an interdisciplinary seminar program on supermarket flow, through which I learned much from David Bell, Yael Benn, Janet Cade, Graham Finlayson, Les Firbank, Ian Jones, Lily Kelting, Ewan Morrison, Angus Young, and Jiachen Zhang. Katharine Carter at Leeds University's Marks and Spencer Archive proved a great help too. I am also grateful for a travel grant from the Lemelson Center for Design and Innovation of the Smithsonian Institution which enabled me to spend a fortnight in the Archives Center and Library of the National Museum of American History. Thank you to Trina Brown, Alison Oswald, Kay Peterson, Jim Roan, and Wendy Shaw for all your interest in this work and for guiding me through such a fascinating range of material. I count myself very lucky indeed to share thoughts and ideas with a range of superb scholars who share my interest in food studies:

Warren Belasco, Tracey Deutsch, Elizabeth Engelhardt, Marcie Cohen Ferris, Sarah Lawson Welsh, Lisa Tolbert, Kyla Wazana Tompkins, and Psyche Williams Forson. I am also very grateful to my three peer reviewers and to Chris Schaberg for all his object lessons and for showing me just how central the cart is in *WALL-E*. Thanks as well to Kate Marshall and Cindy Fulton at the University of California Press, and to Jeff Wyneken for his great sensitivity and patience with the Anglicisms of my original manuscript. I also wish to thank everyone in those audiences in Cambridge, Chapel Hill, Leeds, and Swansea in particular who responded so generously to my various early sketches and musings on "the big shop." The list of gratitude here is long, and probably incomplete, but would certainly include Ned Allen, Kasia Boddy, Hamilton Carroll, Michelle Coghlan, Rachel Farebrother, Max Farrar, Bill Ferris, Mick Gidley, Fiona Green, Bernie Herman, Emily Zobel Marshall, Brendon Nicholls, Caryl Phillips, Greg Radick, Pam Rhodes, Gitanjali Shabani, Mark Taylor-Batty, and Daniel Williams. Last of all, thanks to my wife Sue and our boys Dan and Robbie for keeping it real and ensuring that the trolley has remained, through this project, a familiar part of daily life.

BIBLIOGRAPHY

Abel, Elizabeth. "American Graffiti: The Social Life of Segregation Signs." *African American Review* 42:1 (2008), 9–24.

———. "Bathroom Doors and Drinking Fountains: Jim Crow's Racial Symbolic." *Critical Inquiry* 25:3 (1999), 435–81.

Adorno, Theodor. *Minima Moralia: Reflections on a Damaged Life*, trans. E. F. N. Jephcott (London: Verso, 2005).

Agamben, Giorgio. *Infancy and History: The Destruction of Experience* (London: Verso, 1993).

Alworth, David J. *Site Reading: Fiction, Art, Social Form* (Princeton, NJ: Princeton University Press, 2016).

———. "Supermarket Sociology." *New Literary History* 41:2 (2010), 301–27.

Anderson, Sherwood. *Winesburg, Ohio* (London: Penguin, 1992).

Augé, Marc. *Non-places: Introduction to an Anthropology of Supermodernity*, trans. John Howe (London: Verso, 1995).

Azuchi, Satoshi. *Supermarket*, trans. Paul Warham (New York: St. Martin's Press, 2007).

Bachelard, Gaston. *Poetics of Space* (Boston: Beacon Press, 1994).

Barry, Michael. *The Bon Marché: Bourgeois Culture and the Department Store, 1869–1920* (Princeton, NJ: Princeton University Press, 1981).

Barthes, Roland. "The New Citroën." In *Mythologies,* trans. Annette Lavers (London: Vintage, 2000), 87–90.
Baudrillard, Jean. *America,* trans. Chris Turner (London: Verso, 1988).
———. *The Consumer Society: Myths and Structures,* trans. Chris Turner (Los Angeles: Sage, 1998).
Bauman, Zygmunt. *Consuming Life* (Oxford, UK: Wiley, 2013).
Belasco, Warren. "How Much Depends on Dinner." In *Food Chains: From Farmyard to Shopping Cart,* ed. Warren Belasco and Roger Horowitz (Philadelphia: University of Pennsylvania Press, 2009), 9–16.
———. *Meals to Come: A History of the Future of Food* (Berkeley: University of California Press, 2006).
Benjamin, Walter. "One-Way Street." In *One-Way Street,* trans. Edmund Jephcott and Kingsley Shorter (London: Verso, 1997), 45–107.
———. "The Work of Art in the Age of Mechanical Reproduction." In *One-Way Street and Other Writings,* trans. J. A. Underwood (London: Penguin, 2009), 228–59.
Bennett, Jane. *Vibrant Matter: A Political Ecology of Things* (Durham, NC: Duke University Press, 2010).
Benson, Susan Porter. "The Customers Ain't God: The Work Culture of Department Store Saleswomen." In *Working-Class America: Essays on Labor, Community, and American Society,* ed. Michael H. Frisch and Daniel J. Walkowitz (Urbana: University of Illinois Press, 1983), 185–212.
Beowulf: An Anglo-Saxon Epic Poem, trans. Lesslie Hall (Boston: D.C. Heath, 1892).
Berman, Marshall. *All That Is Solid Melts into Air: The Experience of Modernity* (London: Verso, 1983).
Berridge, Kent C., Chao-Yi Ho, Jocelyn M. Richard, and Alexandra G. DiFeliceantonio. "The Tempted Brain Eats: Pleasure and Desire Circuits in Obesity and Eating Disorders." *Brain Research* 2:1350 (September 2010), 43–64.
Bivens. "Inequality, Exhibit A: Walmart and the Wealth of American Families." Economic Policy Institute. www.epi.org/blog/inequality-exhibit-wal-mart-wealth-american/
Blitz, John H. "Skeuomorphs, Pottery, and Technological Change." *American Anthropologist* 117:4 (2015), 665–78.

Bordo, Susan. *Unbearable Weight: Feminism, Western Culture, and the Body* (Berkeley: University of California Press, 1993).

Bowlby, Rachel. *Carried Away: The Invention of Modern Shopping* (London: Faber and Faber, 2000).

———. *Just Looking: Consumer Culture in Dreiser, Gissing and Zola* (Abingdon, UK: Routledge, 2010).

Boyd, William, and Michael Watts. "Agro-industrial Just in Time: The Chicken Industry and Postwar American Capitalism." In *Globalising Food: Agrarian Questions and Global Restructuring*, ed. David Goodman and Michael Watts (London: Routledge, 1997), 139–65.

Bridge, Gavin. "The Hole World: Scales and Spaces of Extraction." *Scenario* (Autumn 2015).

Brown, Bill. *A Sense of Things: The Object Matter of American Literature* (Chicago: University of Chicago Press, 2003).

Brown, Wendy. "Neoliberalism, Neoconservatism, and De-democratization." *Political Theory* 34:6 (2006), 690–714.

Caro, Robert A. *The Power Broker: Robert Moses and the Gall of New York* (New York: Knopf, 1973).

Cheever, John. "Ocean." In *Collected Stories* (London: Vintage, 2010), 729–50.

Chen, Katherine K. "Prosumption: From Parasitic to Prefigurative." *Sociological Quarterly* 56:3 (2015), 446–59.

Clark, Fred S. *Fitch's List of Super-Markets* (New York: Francis Emory Fitch, 1940).

Cochoy, Franck. "Driving a Shopping Cart from STS to Business, and the Other Way Round: On the Introduction of Shopping Carts in American Grocery Stores (1936–1959)." *Organization* 16:1 (2009), 31–52.

———, and Catherine Grandclément-Chaffy. "Publicizing Goldilocks' Choice at the Supermarket: The Political Work of Shopping Packs, Carts and Talk." In *Making Things Public: Atmospheres of Democracy*, ed. Bruno Latour and Peter Weibel (Cambridge, MA: MIT Press, 2005), 646–57.

Cook, Daniel Thomas. "The Disempowering Empowerment of Children's Consumer 'Choice': Cultural Discourses of the Child Consumer in North America." *Society and Business Review* 2:1 (2007), 35–52.

Crop Production Historical Track Records (Washington, DC: United States Department of Agriculture, 2018).

Cubitt, Sean. "Distribution and Media Flows." *Cultural Politics* 1:2 (2005), 193–214.

Davies, Jeremy. *The Birth of the Anthropocene* (Berkeley: University of California Press, 2016).

De Certeau, Michel. *The Practice of Everyday Life*, trans. Steven Rendall (Berkeley: University of California Press, 1988).

DeLillo, Don. *Americana* (London: Penguin, 1990).

———. *White Noise* (London: Picador, 2011).

Deutsch, Tracey. *Building a Housewife's Paradise: Gender, Politics, and American Grocery Stores in the Twentieth Century* (Chapel Hill: University of North Carolina Press, 2010).

Dipman, Carl. *The Modern Grocery Store* (New York: Butterick, 1931).

Dower, John. *Embracing Defeat: Japan in the Aftermath of World War Two* (London: Penguin, 1999).

Dreiser, Theodore. *Sister Carrie* (Oxford, UK: Oxford University Press, 1998).

Elkin, Stanley. *The Franchiser* (McLean, IL: Dalkey Archive, 2012).

Felski, Rita. "Introduction." *New Literary History* 47:2/3 (2016), 215–27.

Ferris, Marcie Cohen. *The Edible South: The Power of Food and the Making of an American Region* (Chapel Hill: University of North Carolina Press, 2014).

Field, Alexander J. "Economic Growth and Recovery in the United States, 1919–1941." In *The Great Depression of the 1930s: Lessons for Today*, ed. Nicholas Crafts and Peter Fearon (Oxford, UK: Oxford University Press, 2013), 359–94.

———. "The Most Technologically Progressive Decade of the Century." *American Economic Review* 93:4 (2003), 1399–413.

Finlayson, Graham, and Michelle Dalton. "Hedonics of Food Consumption: Are Food 'Liking' and 'Wanting' Viable Targets for Appetite Control in the Obese?" *Current Obesity Reports* 1:1 (2012), 42.

Fisher, Mark. *Capitalist Realism: Is There no Alternative?* (London: Zero Books, 2009).

Flaubert, Gustav. *Madame Bovary* (Oxford, UK: Oxford University Press, 2004).

Freeman, Mike. *Clarence Saunders and the Founding of Piggly Wiggly: The Rise and Fall of a Memphis Maverick* (Charleston, SC: History Press, 2011).

Freidberg, Susanne. *Fresh: A Perishable History* (Cambridge, MA: Harvard University Press, 2009).

Friedberg, Anne. *Window Shopping: Cinema and the Postmodern* (Berkeley: University of California Press, 1994).

Friedman, Milton. *Capitalism and Freedom* (Chicago: University of Chicago Press, 2002).

Fromm, Erich. *Escape from Freedom* (New York: Henry Holt, 1994).

Fruin, John T. *Pedestrian Planning and Design* (Mobile, AL: Elevator World, 1987).

Gardner, John. *Grendel* (London: Vintage, 1989).

Gaskell, Elizabeth. *Sylvia's Lovers* (Oxford, UK: Oxford University Press, 2014).

Gilroy, Paul. *Darker than Blue: On the Moral Economies of Black Atlantic Culture* (Cambridge, MA: Harvard University Press, 2010).

Gram, Malene. "The Supermarket Revisited: Families and Food Shopping." In *The Practice of the Meal: Food, Families and the Market Place,* ed. Benedetta Cappellini, David Marshall, and Elizabeth Parsons (Abingdon, UK: Routledge, 2016), 31–42.

Grandclément. *Wheeling Food Products around the Store … and Away: The Invention of the Shopping Cart, 1936–1953* (Paris: CSI Working Series Papers, 2006). Accessed 26 July 2017 at https://halshs.archives-ouvertes.fr/halshs-00122292v1.

Grandclément-Chaffy, Catherine. "Wheeling One's Groceries around the Store: The Invention of the Shopping Cart, 1936–1953." In *Food Chains: From Farmyard to Shopping Cart,* ed. Warren Belasco and Roger Horowitz (Philadelphia: University of Pennsylvania Press, 2008), 233–52.

Ginsberg, Allen. *Howl and Other Poems* (San Francisco: City Lights, 1956).

Groening, Stephen. "From 'A Box in the Theatre of the World' to the 'World as Your Living Room': Cellular Phones, Television and Mobile Privatization." *New Media and Society* 12:8 (2010), 1331–47.

Hale, Grace. *Making Whiteness: The Culture of Segregation, 1890–1940* (New York: Pantheon, 1998).

Hall, Donald. *The One Day* (Manchester, UK: Carcanet, 1991).

Halper, Emanuel B. *Shopping Center and Store Leases* (New York: Law Journal Press, 2001).
Han, Byung-Chul. *In the Swarm: Digital Prospects,* trans. Erik Butler (Cambridge, MA: MIT Press, 2017).
———. *The Transparency Society,* trans. Erik Butler (Stanford, CA: Stanford University Press, 2015).
Hardt, Michael, and Antonio Negri. *Empire* (Cambridge, MA: Harvard University Press, 2001).
Harris, Neil. *Cultural Excursions: Marketing Appetites and Cultural Tastes in Modern America* (Chicago: University of Chicago Press, 1990).
Herhuth, Eric. "Life, Love, and Programming: The Culture and Politics of *WALL-E* and Pixar Computer Animation." *Cinema Journal* 53:4 (2014), 53–75.
Heywood, John. *The Proverbs of John Heywood,* ed. Julian Sharman (London: George Bell, 1874).
Hodder, Ian. "The Entanglements of Humans and Things: A Long-Term View." *New Literary History* 45:1 (2014), 19–36.
Horkheimer, Max, and Theodor W. Adorno. *Dialectic of Enlightenment: Philosophical Fragments,* trans. Edmund Jephcott (Stanford, CA: Stanford University Press, 2002).
Hyman, Louis. *Debtor Nation: The History of America in Red Ink* (Princeton, NJ: Princeton University Press, 2011).
Jackson, John Brickerhoff. *Discovering the Vernacular Landscape* (New Haven, CT: Yale University Press, 1984).
Jackson, Peter. *Anxious Appetites: Food and Consumer Culture* (London: Bloomsbury, 2015).
Jackson, Shirley. *Hangsaman* (London: Penguin, 2013).
James, Henry. *The Golden Bowl,* ed. Philip Horne (London: Penguin, 2009).
Jameson, Fredric. *Valences of the Dialectic* (London: Verso, 2009).
Johnson, Fred W. *Shoplifter Racket: Tricks of the Trade.* Acme Supermarkets, 1953. http://collections.si.edu/search/results.htm
Katti, Christian S.G., and Bruno Latour. "Mediating Political 'Things,' and the Forked Tongue of Modern Culture: A Conversation with Bruno Latour." *Art Journal* 65:1 (Spring 2006), 94–115.

Kearful, Frank. "Alimentary Poetics: Robert Lowell and Allen Ginsberg." *Partial Answers: Journal of Literature and the History of Ideas* 11:1 (2013), 87–108.

Kholod, Marina, Keiji Takai, and Katutoshi Yada. "Clockwise and Anti-clockwise Directions of Customer Orientation in a Supermarket: Evidence from RFID Data." In *Knowledge-Based and Intelligent Information and Engineering Systems*, ed. Randy Goebel, Jörg Siekmann, and Wolfgang Wahlster (Heidelberg, Germany: Springer, 2011), 304–9.

Klein, Naomi. *No Logo: Taking Aim at the Brand Bullies* (London: Picador, 1999).

Kracaeur, Siegfried. *The Mass Ornament: Weimar Essays,* trans. Thomas Y. Levin (Cambridge, MA: Harvard University Press, 1995).

Latour, Bruno. *An Inquiry into Modes of Existence: An Anthropology of the Moderns,* trans. Catherine Porter (Cambridge, MA: Harvard University Press, 2013).

———. "Morality and Technology: The End of the Means." *Theory, Culture and Society* 19:5/6 (2002), 247–60.

———. *Reassembling the Social: An Introduction to Actor-Network Theory* (Oxford, UK: Oxford University Press, 2005).

———. *We Have Never Been Modern,* trans. Catherine Porter (Cambridge, MA: Harvard University Press, 1993).

———, Graham Harman, and Peter Erdélyi. *The Prince and the Wolf: Latour and Harman at the LSE* (Winchester: Zero Books, 2011).

Ledermann, Robert P. *Christmas on State Street: 1940s and Beyond* (Charleston, SC: Arcadia, 2002).

Lefebvre, Henri. *Critique of Everyday Life: The One Volume Edition,* trans. Gregory Elliott (London: Verso, 2002).

Levin, Ira. *The Stepford Wives* (London: Corsair, 2011).

Lofland, Lyn H. *A World of Strangers: Order and Action in Urban Public Space* (New York: Basic Books, 1973).

Longstreth, Richard. *The Department Store Transformed, 1920–1960* (New Haven, CT: Yale University Press, 2010).

———. *The Drive-In, the Supermarket, and the Transformation of Commercial Space in Los Angeles, 1914–1941* (Cambridge, MA: MIT Press, 1999).

Lordon, Frédéric. *Willing Slaves of Capitalism: Spinoza and Marx on Desire*, trans. Gabriel Ash (London: Verso, 2014).
Mack, Adam. "'Speaking of Tomatoes': Supermarkets, The Senses, and Sexual Fantasy in Modern America." *Journal of Social History* 43:4 (July 2010), 815–42.
Martin, Shannon E., and Kathleen A. Hansen. *Newspapers of Record in a Digital Age: From Hot Type to Hot Link* (Westport, CT: Praeger, 1998).
Mayo, James. *The American Grocery Store* (Westport, CT: Greenwood, 1993).
McAusland, Randolph. *Supermarkets: Fifty Years of Progress* (Washington, DC: Food Marketing Institute, 1980).
McCarthy, Cormac. *The Road* (London: Random House, 2006).
Michaels, Walter Benn. "*Sister Carrie*'s Popular Economy." *Critical Inquiry* 7:2 (Winter 1980), 373–90.
Miller, Daniel. *A Theory of Shopping* (London: Polity, 1998).
Mintz, Sidney W. *Sweetness and Power: The Place of Sugar in Modern History* (New York: Penguin, 1986).
Mirrlees, Tanner. "Hollywood's Uncritical Dystopias." *CineAction* 95 (December 2015), 4–12.
Montague, Julian. *The Stray Shopping Carts of Eastern North America: A Guide to Field Identification* (New York: Abrams Image, 2006).
Mumford, Lewis. *The City in History: Its Origins, Its Transformations and Its Prospects* (London: Penguin, 1991).
———. *The Culture of Cities* (London: Secker and Warburg, 1944).
———. *Technics and Civilization* (New York: Harbinger, 1963).
Mussell, James. *Science, Time and Space in the Late Nineteenth Century Periodical Press: Movable Types* (London: Ashgate, 2007).
Ngai, Sianne. *Ugly Feelings* (Cambridge, MA: Harvard University Press, 2007).
Nojeim, Michael J. *Gandhi and King: The Power of Nonviolent Resistance* (Westport, CT: Praeger, 2004).
Nora, Pierre. "Between Memory and History: Les Lieux des Mémoire." *Representations* 26 (1989), 7–24.
Norris, Frank. *The Pit* (Chicago: Doubleday, 1903).
Now a Modern Foodstore: As Easy as ABC (Aurora, IL: Lyon Metal Products, 1938).

Nye, David E. *American Technological Sublime* (Cambridge, MA: MIT Press, 1994).
Ogden, Cynthia, Margaret D. Carroll, Katherine M. Flegal, and Cheryl D. Fryar. *Mean Body Weight, Height, and Body Mass Index, United States 1960–2002* (Hyattsville, MD: Centers for Disease Control and Prevention, 2004). Accessed 8 September 2017 at www.cdc.gov/nchs/data/ad/ad347.pdf.
Orleck, Annelise. *Common Sense and a Little Fire: Women and Working-Class Politics in the United States, 1900–1965* (Chapel Hill: University of North Carolina Press, 1995).
Packard, Vance. *The Hidden Persuaders* (New York: Ig, 2007).
Palley, Thomas I. "The Economics and Political Economy of Milton Friedman: An Old Keynesian Critique." In *Milton Friedman: Contributions to Economics and Public Economy*, ed. Robert A. Cord and J. Daniel Hammond (Oxford, UK: Oxford University Press, 2006), 632–55.
Percy, Walker. *The Moviegoer* (York, UK: Methuen, 2013).
Potter, David M. *People of Plenty: Economic Abundance and the American Character* (Chicago: University of Chicago Press, 1958).
Robertson, Ritchie. *Mock-Epic Poetry from Pope to Heine* (Oxford, UK: Oxford University Press, 2009).
Robin, Corey. *The Reactionary Mind: Conservatism from Edmund Burke to Sarah Palin* (Oxford, UK: Oxford University Press, 2011).
Sen, Amartya. *Poverty and Famines: An Essay on Entitlement and Deprivation* (Oxford, UK: Oxford University Press, 1983).
Sennett, Richard. *The Fall of Public Man* (London: Penguin, 1976).
Shaviro, Steven. "Capitalist Monsters." *Historical Materialism* 10:4 (2002), 281–90.
———. *Post-Cinematic Affect* (Ropley, UK: Zero Book, 2010).
Simonis, Doris (ed.). *Inventors and Inventions*. Vol. 5 (New York: Marshall Cavendish, 2008).
Spencer, Elizabeth. *The Snare* (Jackson, MI: Banner Books, 1993).
Spufford, Francis. *Red Plenty* (London: Faber, 2010).
Steinbeck, John. *Sweet Thursday* (London: Penguin, 2000).
Strasser, Susan. "Woolworth to Wal-Mart: Mass Merchandising and the Changing Culture of Consumption." In *Wal-Mart: The Face of*

Twenty-First-Century Capitalism, ed. Nelson Lichtenstein (New York: New Press, 2006), 31–56.

Surdam, David George. *Century of the Leisured Masses: Entertainment and the Transformation of Twentieth-Century America* (New York: Oxford University Press, 2015).

Tolbert, Lisa. "'The Aristocracy of the Market Basket': Self-Service Food Shopping in the New South." In *Food Chains: From Farmyard to Shopping Cart*, ed. Warren Belasco and Roger Horowitz (Philadelphia: University of Pennsylvania Press, 2009), 179–95.

———. "Beyond Piggly Wiggly: A Cultural History of the Self-Service Store" (unpublished manuscript, 2018).

Trachtenberg, Alan. *Reading American Photographs: Images as History, Mathew Brady to Walker Evans* (New York: Hill and Wang, 1989).

Tressler, Donald K. *The Freezing Preservation of Fruits, Juices and Vegetables* (New York: Avi, 1936).

Twitchell, James B. *Living It Up: Our Love Affair with Luxury* (New York: Columbia University Press, 2011).

Urry, John. "Inhabiting the Car." *Sociological Review* 54:1 (2006), 17–31.

Veblen, Thorstein. *Theory of the Leisure Class* (Mineola, NY: Dover Thrift, 1994).

Vizenor, Gerald. *The Trickster of Liberty: Native Heirs to a Wild Baronage* (Norman: University of Oklahoma Press, 2005).

Wells, Christopher W. *Car Country: An Environmental History* (Seattle: University of Washington Press, 2012).

Wik, Reynold M. "Review of *Fordson, Farmall, and Poppin' Johnny: A History of the Farm Tractor and Its Impact on America* by Robert C. Williams." *Isis* 78:4 (1987), 626.

Williams, Raymond. *Keywords: A Vocabulary of Culture and Society* (New York: Oxford University Press, 1983).

———. *The Long Revolution* (Peterborough, ON: Broadview, 1985).

———. *Towards 2000* (London: Chatto and Windus, 1983).

Wilson, Terry P. *The Cart That Changed the World: The Career of Sylvan N. Goldman* (Norman: University of Oklahoma Press, 1978).

Zimmerman, Max M. *The Super Market: A Revolution in Distribution* (New York: McGraw-Hill, 1955).

———. "The Supermarket and the Changing Retail Structure." *Journal of Advertising* 5:4 (1941), 402–9.

PATENTS

Goldman, Sylvan N. *Combination Basket and Carriage,* US2155896. 4 May 1937.
———. *Folding Basket Carriage for Self-Service Stores,* US2196914. 14 March 1938.
———. *Child Seat for Store Service Carriers.* US2662775A. 15 September 1950.
Saunders, Clarence. *Self-Serving Store.* US1242872. 21 October 1916.

DISCOGRAPHY

Eugene McDaniels. "Supermarket Blues." In *Headless Heroes of the Apocalypse* (Atlantic, 1971).
The Clash. "Lost in the Supermarket." In *London Calling* (CBS, 1979).

TV AND FILMOGRAPHY

The Big Sick, dir. Michael Showalter (FilmNation, 2017).
Ipcress File, dir. Sidney J. Furie (Lowndes, 1965).
The Last Testament: The Making of 'London Calling,' dir. Don Letts (Sony, 2004).
The Pervert's Guide to Ideology, dir. Sophie Fiennes (Zeitgeist, 2012).
WALL-E, dir. Andrew Stanton (Disney, 2008).
"Wanna Partner?" In *The Good Wife,* episode 22, season 6, dir. Robert King (CBS, 2015).

INDEX

Amazon, 1–2, 8–9, 14–16
Anthropocene. *See* environment
Augé, Marc, 50, 106–7

barcodes, 3, 48–50, 103
Bauman, Zygmunt, 143n38
Benjamin, Walter, 96–98
Bezos, Jeffrey, 1–2, 8–9, 14–16
Bordo, Susan, 42

capitalism, 15, 49–50, 52, 94–95, 113, 124; and desire, 115–17, 134n13
car culture: analogies with the supermarket, 13, 36, 44–45, 88, 108–10; post-war domination of, 74–77, 81–82; rise of between the wars, 19–20, 62
cellophane, 60, 91–92, 119. *See also* packaging
Cheever, John, 81
children, 3, 41, 58, 68–72, 83, 86, 97–101, 108
Cochoy, Frank, 16–17, 50, 69
communism, 85–87, 88, 94

consumers: children as, 3, 68–72, 83, 86, 108; compared to customers, 115–17; new tactile modes of, 29, 30–33, 92–94; predictable genres of, 48–50, 54–56, 106, 107, 110; rise to dominance of, 14–15, 16, 24, 26, 27, 37, 95, 106, 109
convenience, 5, 38–39, 45, 54, 79, 122
crime. *See* surveillance
Cullen, Michael, 43–44, 51, 53, 54, 78, 133n45

Deutsch, Tracey, 17, 32, 86
digital culture. *See* online shopping
Dipman, Carl, 55, 130n4
Dreiser, Theodore, 22–24, 56, 57, 128n5, 129n12

ecology. *See* environment
Elkin, Stanley, 104–5, 113
environment, 119–24

159

Fisher, Mark, 15, 134 n13
Flaubert, Gustav, 21
flow: clockwise and counterclockwise floorplans, 56, 136n30; continuing use of distraction and deceleration, 39, 55–58; food distribution and, 37, 52–53, 56–58, 93; in store "just in time" distribution, 53, 54, 59; and packaging and ad design, 91–93

Gardner, John, 110–14, 120
Gaskell, Elizabeth, 21
gender. *See* housewife stereotype
Ginsberg, Allen, 17, 65
glass: compared to cellophane, 91–92; gradual replacement of, 30, 91; in Victorian shop displays, 23–24
globalization, 15–16, 42, 50, 74, 106, 116, 120–24; as a planned "natural" phenomenon, 78, 88, 90–95; of the shopping cart, 83–88, 140n1
Goldman Sachs, 1
Goldman, Sylvan, 20, 78, 81, 83, 94; creates cart with Fred Young, 60–64, 89, 137n9; expands business nationwide, 70–73; opportunism, 73–74; promotes cart to customers, 66–69, 84
Grandclément-Chaffy, Catherine, 16–17, 66–67, 71, 73, 74

housewife stereotype, 3–4, 13, 30, 34, 39–42, 52, 55; paradoxes of, 42, 57–58, 90–91
hunger, 21, 42, 62, 72, 111; redefined under the supermarket system, 121–22

individualism, 18, 29, 49, 54–56, 59, 79, 88, 94, 106, 107, 110
internet. *See* online shopping

Jackson, Shirley, 65

Khrushchev, Nikita, 85–86
King Kullen. *See* Cullen, Michael

Landor, Walter, 89–94, 103
Latour, Bruno, 46–50, 65, 70, 73, 93, 107, 108, 109
Life magazine, 2–4, 49, 84

McCarthy, Cormac, 6, 95–96, 98–101, 104, 120
Mikoyan, Anastas, 86–88
Moses, Robert, 44, 80, 85
Mumford, Lewis, 62, 65, 124, 133n46

neoliberalism, 14–15, 94–95, 119–20
Newman, Arnold, 3–4

obesity, 68–69, 77–82, 122–24. *See also* overeating
online shopping, 2, 5–6, 8–10, 14–16, 97–98, 119
overeating, 2–4, 68–69, 111–16. *See also* obesity

patents and patenting, 9, 34–38, 60, 64, 68–69, 70–73, 85, 89, 94
packaging, 60, 86, 91–92, 105, 119, 120
Piggly Wiggly. *See* Saunders, Clarence
Presley, Elvis, 104
Progressive Grocer, 12, 54, 55, 69, 130n4

race: and African American "spokeservants," 41, 58; and African Americans, 40–41, 42,

104; assumed whiteness of supermarket customers, 39–42, 43, 58, 78, 104; and segregation, 39–41
Reagan, Ronald, 95
refrigeration: domestic, 2, 20, 59, 62, 81, 124; commercial, 17, 38, 40, 59, 61–62, 65, 81, 87, 88, 91; in food distribution system, 52

Saturday Evening Post, 68, 84
Saunders, Clarence, 13, 51, 55, 60, 61, 78, 83; newspaper promotions of, 38–40; self-service patents of, 34–36, 70–71; and view of white femininity, 39–43
Self, Will, 7–8
self-service, 13, 19–21; early development of, 26–30, 38–40, 42–45, 52, 57–58; international popularization of, 60–61, 65, 71, 73, 83
shoplifting. *See* surveillance
skeumorphism: definition of, 7; digital revival of, 7–9; and hunger, 120–21; and the shopping cart, 8–10, 14–16
Soviet Union, 88, 94
Steinbeck, John, 62
suburbs and suburbanization, 1, 2, 6, 44–45, 62, 74, 80–82, 83, 104, 140n1

sugar, 51, 52, 72, 80, 108, 119–20, 123, 124
supermarket: and consumer behaviour, 46–49, 56–58, 59; evolution in the United States, 41–45, 51–55, 71, 78–79, 90–93, 103–5; and introduction of shopping cart, 60–67; spread outside United States, 83–88, 140n1. *See also* flow; globalization; self-service; textuality
surveillance, 17, 24, 32–33, 57, 131n18, 127–8n1

theft. *See* surveillance

Universal Product Code. *See* barcodes

Watson, Orla E., 20, 73–76, 89
WALL-E, 122–23
Walmart, 78, 113
Whole Foods, 10, 15
whiteness. *See* race
Williams, Raymond, 103–4, 106–7, 115–16, 120, 122
Windows. *See* glass

Young, Fred W., 20, 60, 62, 64–66, 68, 71, 73, 89

Žižek, Slavoj, 100, 118

www.ingramcontent.com/pod-product-compliance
Lightning Source LLC
Chambersburg PA
CBHW031454160426
43195CB00010BB/969